The Digital Worker

Leveraging New Technology: RPA

Convention Edition

Douglas Erb

Co-Contributors Mark Warne, Ben Cordner,

& Elizabeth Dennett

The Digital Worker: Leveraging New Technology: RPA

Published by:

Lanshore Publications
1795 N Fry Suite 289
Katy, TX77449, USA

Address all inquiries to:

info@lanshore.com

ISBN: 978-1-7379705-0-7

Editor and Interior Layout Design: Amy Rice

Cover Designer: Susanne Branston

Every attempt has been made to source properly all quotes.

Printed in the United States of America

First Edition

"There's a lot of automation that can happen that isn't a replacement of humans but of mind-numbing behavior."

Stewart Butterfield

Contents

Introduction

UiPath CEO, Daniel Dines, said something revolutionary: "If Bill Gates said, 'a computer on every desk,' our vision is to have one robot for every person." It sounded incredibly sci-fi a handful of years ago, but now it is a reality speeding toward revolutionizing workplaces and homes. All you have to do is call up Siri or Alexa for proof of concept.

Robotic Process Automation (RPA) is necessary in the business world today and has been seeping into daily life at all levels, whether people recognize they are utilizing RPA or not. RPA is software programmed to perform rule-based tasks without human intervention—across multiple applications and processes. RPA can handle transactions, triggering responses, manipulating data, communicating with other digital systems to build cohesive movement of data and information within and connected to the primary organization. While all of that is the operating premise of this book, we will explore the different ways that works and looks to give you an idea of the options RPA can offer your organization to make processes run smoothly to optimize every area of potentiality within your organization.

We will explore the applications in use currently and how businesses can adopt practices that will give them the ability to be more efficient in their goals immediately. Utilizing tools to enhance efficiency and optimize the productivity of key employees will change the way businesses operate.

If you are in the planning stages of your business, this exploration into RPA could be the ultimate game changer. It's easier to begin with great processes than get key players to adopt and implement change. With the right tools, even established businesses can adopt new technologies to become more competitive. If you have already started your business, this is still for you.

The goal is always to optimize the bottom line without sacrificing client/customer satisfaction or destroying morale within the ranks. We will help you plan and design a Digital Worker to take the monotonous robotic processes off the desks of your MVPs so they can focus on the objectives that keep them excited about showing up for work, which creates more space for success for everyone.

The first step to solving any problem is acknowledging and defining the problem. For instance, does it take three or more employees to file and crosscheck invoices, incoming and outgoing payments, checked against bank accounts, making sure invoices are being tracked, correctly marked paid or unpaid, with reminders sent out? When bills are sent out, there are incoming calls with questions or explanations which require additional employees to answer phones with subsequent questions and concerns. A CPA may need to double and triple check multiple registers from multiple employees and clients. Already, this process dealing with invoices is too long and involved!

What if there was a way for a digital worker to consolidate the processes, sending reports to the CPA, and anyone else that needed the reports to complete their work? Human interaction with the program would only be necessary when the digital worker wasn't able to rectify a process. What if this system digitized concerns and streamlined calls, by creating an easy-to-use system for billing, that clients and customers preferred to waiting on hold for a human? This would require less manpower for the mundane tasks, less errors would occur, clients and customers would be handled by less employees causing less frustration and runaround for answers.

The digital worker exists as a personal assistant and asset to your employees and customers. When you know better, you can do better. Digital Workers will give you the tools to enhance your client, customer, and employee experience. Imagine a staff that is invigorated, instead of worn down, every day they walked in the door. Where would your team take your company if the digital worker was doing the monotonous work?

This book also serves to show the visionary ways that RPA can be utilized in different fields from business to government agencies to the medical world. Lanshore has kicked around ideas that could be life saving and changing in certain fields, and we debut our teams innovative brainstorming process using data and real-life scenarios that can be improved upon using RPA. We would love to see the Digital Worker helping to transform lives on ethical levels as well as maximizing workflow and transitioning companies to more successful ways of operating.

Chapter I

The Beginning of an Industry

Vision and innovation go hand in hand.
Great leaders create opportunities.

Vision and innovation go hand in hand. Good leaders jump on board when opportunities present themselves. Great leaders create opportunities. We will take a quick look at industry predictions and quotes that are laughable because they were clearly wrong. The chairman of IBM, Thomas Watson, said, "I think there's a world market for maybe five computers."[1] When he said this in 1943, computers were still huge, so the market for what he could see was a small market. In 1977, Ken Olsen said, "There is no reason anyone would want a computer in their home."[2] Now, you'd be hard pressed to find a home without a computer. The end of the internet was predicted in 1995; Apple was declared dead in 1997, Bill Gates figured spam would disappear in 2004. Paul Krugman declared this is 1998: "By 2005 or so, it will be clear that the Internet's impact on the economy has been no greater than the fax machine's."[2] *BusinessWeek* reported in 1975 that offices would be paperless by the 1990's due to digitization. Yet, offices are using more than 12 trillion pieces of paper each year.[3] That's more paper than before digitizing offices. What do all of these bad predictions tell us? Maybe, to shut our mouths, or maybe not to trust limiting progress with forecasts.

There's a tug-of-war with progress. Nostalgic rumination like "back in my day" logically reeks. Back in the day, the life expectancy was much lower; people only traveled inside a twenty-to-thirty-mile radius; typhoid and the black death took out cities; you could only eat what you grew; access to clean water or medical help was non-existent, we could go on. Progress requires us to keep up or move out of the way. The library thought the card catalogue filing cabinets were there to stay. Now, it's all digitized. The online landscape has taken over shopping, education, bill pay, banking, and more. The digital world is taking another massive leap forward, as the foundation for what's going to rapidly evolve next is already firmly in place. That is what this book is all about: Innovation in robotic processes automation, which we will refer to as RPA throughout the book.

Sitting in a room with many of my fellow industry professionals, having just watched Dr. Michio Kaku give a presentation about advancements in intelligence, my mind started racing about the future of technology and the workplace. Afterwards, discussion in the room reflected the innovative way the future would need to be approached. Just like there was a race to the moon, there is a race between industries to level up for the money that is spent by consumers and clients in their field.

The fastest way to lose is to not realize there is a race. The second fastest way to lose is to lag behind competitors in advancing processes. The processes that can be improved upon easiest is the repetitive processes that computers can manage, freeing up humans to do the things computers cannot. My interest became training the computers. How would we shape the future? How could we advance the industry? What does the world look like as we give more and more responsibility to computers?

The more we consider the advancement of technology, the broader concerns become: What about ethical agreement standards? What constitutes agreement when computers are in charge of processes? Does it matter? Does higher efficiency of processes cut jobs? Is that ethical? It ensures more profitability. Putting profitability before people might help a company endure, but how do we safeguard standards of living as computers take over repetitive jobs?

Peers meandered out of the conference and went their own way, figuring out what the new insights meant to them. For me, the journey into Artificial Intelligence (AI) was being expanded upon. Now, I was aware of what existed. The deep dive into human psychology and behavior had to merge with the possibilities that AI was offering. The expansion of knowledge required a look into all intelligence: Why humans do what they do, how the decisions shape the processes, logic versus emotion, the questions rising up seemed endless.

Time was consumed reading books by psychologists, physicists, mathematicians, business gurus, anyone that was an expert in their field and could shed light on humanity and nuances of life. Michael Lewis was one of my favorites. I had been discussing *The Money Ball* since it had come out, piquing my interest in human behavior management by utilizing monetary reward. Regularly, his quotes would flow from my mouth in meetings like I was responsible for the content. His book, *The Undoing Project*, began my quest into Artificial Intelligence.

To start at the beginning, you have come to the right place. While delving into AI is exciting, it can also be overwhelming to process the vastness that is encompassed by the possibilities. RPA (Robotic Process Automation) is the beginning of the AI spectrum. Automating human processes by regulating the movement and flow of information removes the mundane repetitive work of certain jobs, streamlining the processes for less margin of error and faster execution. While RPA doesn't learn, it is necessary as a first step for building systems that will integrate the future of AI as it becomes available.

RPA CAPABILITIES

Whether you are aware of this or not, RPA is an active part of your day. We will talk more about that later. Right now, let's walk through a normal workday to see what RPA can do for an organization on the ground level: You come to the office and boot up your computer, if it isn't already on. Your digital worker (robot) immediately begins work as your assistant: Generating invoices; scanning your emails and prioritizing them for your attention; looking at contracts for key issues or responses; balancing bank accounts to the available accounting, etc. Your digital worker will interact and make recommendations or simply do the work it's been given permission to perform on your behalf. Instead of a personal assistant that needs guidance and verbal interaction to complete tasks, the Digital Worker is programmed to perform various and numerous rule-based operations that itemize and prioritize different tasks in order for the human worker to have time for things that are more important and satisfying than running checks and balances on numbers that span multiple programs etc.

If you were hiring a person, what would you teach them? What processes would you want to offload so you could get to the more meaningful work more quickly? How could your work output look with a more thorough eye and consistency? This is not a critique of what you do or how you accomplish it. Imagine you didn't have to scroll through 250 emails every morning because your digital worker flagged the client and superior officer emails. Your responses would be timely, and the email portion of your morning could become mere minutes instead of over an hour. What would you do with that extra time?

John Kenneth Galbraith made a great point: "Clearly the most unfortunate people are those who must do the same thing over and over again, every minute, or perhaps twenty to the minute. They deserve the shortest hours and the highest pay." The business model of the past and present has processes that require an employee to perform mundane tasks repetitively, but companies do not compensate these performers the way Galbraith suggests.

Freeing up employees with the attention to detail these tasks require could add a lot to the overall health of an organization, saving training time from the revolving door of seat warmers that could never be satisfied to be stuck at that job until retirement. The next generation surely doesn't have the patience of the former generations when it comes to performing repetitive tasks at an hourly rate. This is where Robotic Process Automation is worth it's human counterpart's weight in gold. Reinventing a workplace where the focus is on innovation and driving the company toward goals and visions that were once only dreams is becoming possible with RPA handling the details of the mundane tasks, freeing payroll hours to be delegated to much more important things than reconciling paperwork printed from online files to other online databases.

Not many children have gone to 'Career Day' in elementary school and declared their future dream job as data entry, professed their clerical aspirations, or reconciling data as what gets them excited to grow up. The digital worker has yet to evolve into an entity that complains about the monotonous work. Whatever the robot equivalent to going home to drown in a bottle and sorrow hasn't been kicked back in data streams as of yet, so it is safe to assume that RPA is satisfied with what most humans dread. I say most, because assuredly, there will be someone that wants to email me about their love for repetitious work. There is nothing wrong with the work, that isn't what this book is about. This book is about giving people the knowledge to advance processes as they are comfortable. The early adopters will reap the benefits over their peers that wait. That's just a fact. When you know better, you do better. RPA is better and a step forward.

Welcome to the creation of the Digital Worker.

In the past few years, Robotic Process Automation (RPA) has moved rapidly from being a niche technology to becoming recognized as a major driver of economic performance. Three key technical foundations, dating back several decades, have allowed for the seemingly rapid emergence of RPA.

THE FOUNDATIONS

The first key advancement on the road to RPA is screen/web scraping technologies, the origins of which date back to the 1980's. Originally developed to facilitate the linking of new computer systems with older 'legacy' systems, screen/web scraping was updated in the 1990's and early 2000's to perform automated gathering of data from webpages.

The second key foundation was Workflow Automation Software. This advancement automatically triggered a process of steps in response to some input, such as a user's actions or a web form being completed. The use of Workflow Automation Software has come a long way with developed easy-to-use visual tools. The prompting on the screen makes each step of the process streamlined, regardless of the user, which ensures each step is completed before moving on to the next screen.

The third key foundation is Artificial Intelligence. AI was founded as an academic discipline in 1956 but has only recently begun to yield practical tools and uses: Optical character recognition, human speech recognition, ability to identify particular types of images (i.e., tumors).

THE CATALYST

At the same time as these foundation technologies were being developed, the big trend in information technology was for enormous, all-encompassing Enterprise Resource Planning (ERP) systems, implemented at vast expense and not always successful. Or, if an organization didn't want to go down the ERP road, they invested millions developing interfaces between their disparate computer systems, needing expert programmers skilled in multiple languages and, again, not always ending in success.

With that as the backdrop, the time was ripe for someone to develop a piece of non-invasive software, something not requiring changes to the underlying computer systems, that would allow an organization to replicate the behavior of a human operator. There were already robots that could press steel, rivet, or weld, why couldn't there be a robot that emulated the behavior of a person on a computer? And so, from the combination of screen scraping, workflow automation and artificial intelligence, Robotic Process Automation was born in the early 2000s.

DOUG'S STORY

Focusing on RPA wasn't part of the original plan when I entered the world of technology. Over twenty years ago, my start was in consulting in the commissions' management niche (or as we like to say, the evaluation of monetary and non-monetary rewards on human behavior). The focus was managing large scale sales' forces for large companies. Instead of the company managing the mathematics and figures, we handled that. Commission software opened the door with a vendor partner.

There was always a nagging that something was lacking when I was presenting solutions to clients. Most clients desired to make their life easier, but after implementing a system they seemed to be stuck with something that was more complex than what they originally started with. Often times they would end up with something that wasn't as efficient either, but because they spent so much time and effort in putting the new system in place, they had to use it. When I attended a conference on pay management (credit card processing and such) that was recommended by some of my IBM partner colleagues, in 2016, surprise set in as I attended seminars on machine learning and ethical AI. Michio Kaku, renowned physicist, opened my mind to the additional possibilities within the world of commissions management as I listened to him discuss AI applications.

As I started to research further into AI, it came to my attention that many people tried to dive into AI for the sake of it, and that there were logical steps prior to doing this. These logical steps, understanding business need and process drove me to starting to research more about RPA.

With the great minds at Lanshore, RPA became a creation lab for helping companies, universities, governments, and any other public serving entity where the only limits were what processes could be optimized and automated. We keep pushing that limit looking for a better way, it's more than just nuances. We broadened the spectrum as part of the plan for all organizations. The question that I have set out to find an answer to is this: What does the optimal digital worker look like? With human guides to manage the digital worker, what can be overcome and streamlined for more productivity and better results? Throughout the rest of this book, we will explore the capabilities, problems, and exciting opportunities that the digital worker affords the adopters of this technology.

This is just the beginning, that's the exciting news.

Chapter 2

AI/RPA: Evolution or Revolution?

What could you automate in your daily life? If you answered 'nothing,' you might be surprised to find you are already using AI and/or RPA regularly.

Let's talk about your calendar. Maybe, you take a karate (or dance class, anything really) that has five offerings for the level you want to specifically attend. The class may have a calendar invite required for the school's planning. If one class is booked, you want to make the next available class. You could go look at your calendar, figure out when there is time free, find the corresponding class, create a block on the calendar, submit the request to be added to the class to the school, and wait for confirmation on the request before knowing whether another time needs to be requested.

Automating the calendar through RPA is easy because there is a ruleset to scheduling. You set the rules that need executed (Karate class on Tuesday and Thursday). You give access to your calendar and link the karate school calendar, giving permission for the program to choose certain classes based on a hierarchy and availability to both schedules. This could be set weekly or only when you go in to make changes. So, your digital assistant would start the weekly planning on Friday nights, if that's when you set it to run, for the next week.

The digital assistant then works like this: "Okay, based on these criteria, I'm going to go ahead in creating a block of time for this class. I will email the karate instructor, submit the registration for attending this first-choice spot in the class. Once the confirmation email is received, I confirm the calendar block and send you a reminder."

A digital assistant can run many rule-based activities for you. The downfall would be if something happens (you get in a car wreck or have a family emergency), the robot doesn't know that information. When there is a disruption in life, you have to manually cancel events and stall the digital assistant. It isn't so difficult to change, but if you decided to take two months off classes and don't turn off the digital assistant, you will be scheduled and not showing up. That might be better than never getting into the classes you want because you procrastinate sending the request.

On a business scale, scheduling several fifteen-minute calls and meetings throughout the day gets much easier when you can send a link for people to schedule themselves and use the master schedule to see open windows of time and keep confirmed appointments. The process sounds in-depth written out, but the good news is the available programs only need you to click certain boxes and permissions, you just reap the benefits.

This chapter will handle some of the technical aspects of RPA—the evolution or revolution of the technology. It's important to know how and why the Digital Worker produces the results it does. The value of having information helps turn knowledge into earning power across the board.

THE UNIVERSAL PROOF OF USE

A lot of people will hear about artificial intelligence or automation and think they have no use for it, "I am never going to use that!" Naysayers might say they don't use smartphones, or it seems like too much effort for something they already do without the use of technology. Here's the proof that many people are already using AI: "Hey, Siri!" "Alexa!" "Using Google talk to text to search the internet, "Google, who batted in behind Hank Aaron in the World Series?" "Siri, set a timer for me for 3 pm." "Alexa, play 'Baby Shark.'"

Not everyone is using the calendar RPA I mentioned before, but it isn't far off. My grandma has a smart phone, so that excuse doesn't always fly—there's no longer an age barrier to technology.

My wife is not an avid technologist like me, but she will still use Siri to set timers, call people, send messages. "Siri, send message to Doug to pick up milk on his way home." Siri can access and set my calendar using RPA. The

People that once had no interest or use for these technologies are seeing how their lives can be improved by implementing what is available. There are refrigerators available now that can give you video access to the contents (helping catch who puts the empty containers back in or more likely look at what you might need while already at the store). Some of these new refrigerators will generate a shopping list. There are recipe sites that generate shopping lists while some take it further: If you are trying to use up ingredients, you can tell the site what you have on hand, and they will match you to new recipes to try, even if you have dietary needs (diabetes, gluten-free, allergies accounted for). The possibilities with new technologies are endless.

MACHINE LEARNING

Machine learning (ML) is a portion of artificial intelligence known as Specified AI. The ability to take an individual process and infer decisions. Machine learning uses algorithms and statistical models to perform a specific task, without using explicit instructions, rules or models, relying on patterns and inference instead. When applied to business problems, machine learning can also be referred to as predictive analytics.

Use of machine learning begins with having a defined problem or a defined process that's to be addressed. The next step is to translate the problem definition into an algorithm that can be implemented in software. Once the algorithm has been implemented, the final step is to provide the data set and the data sampling that will be used to “train” the system.

Let's look at radiology as an example. Radiologists have to look over scans and x-rays all day to recognize issues within the black and white scans of the human body to send detailed reports to doctors to assist them in the correct diagnosis of their patients. In the medical world, the earlier an issue is caught, the more effective treatment can be. AI could be implemented here and be taught with thousands of scans to catch variances and abnormalities in scans to alert radiologist's attention to somewhere on a scan that they may have missed. For instance, patient is presenting with stomach pain, so the focus is the stomach whereas machine learning has helped the bot pick up on cancerous cells in the chest, alerting the radiologist to somewhere they may not have been looking for an issue. Human error isn't always malicious, it can be from patient led focus. The bot isn't affected by the emotions a patient may present, or other cues that we take in, the bot is just looking for incongruities. That's its job. Machine learning for the benefit of the patient, to alert the radiologist of its findings, only enhances the probability that nothing is missed in a scan. The radiologist still has to review the anomalies and write a report of findings to the doctor, and the radiologist would be reviewing the bot's findings. The machine and human work together to the advantage of the patient.

ARTIFICIAL INTELLIGENCE

Artificial Intelligence covers a broad spectrum. We define it here as anything from RPA (process mapping and execution) to General AI such as neural networks. As we define General AI, it does not exist on a human level. If we think about how people define AI it is the ability to learn tasks, such as cancer identification in an x-ray or scan. AI will have to read through thousands of x-rays and scans to acquire the ability and accuracy to start functioning but will eventually learn to narrow in on diagnosis within a reasonable error limit, much like a human who goes to school.

The algorithms that exist for artificial intelligence have largely been developed by a couple of companies, many alongside university or higher education groups. These algorithms can be basic, such as a linear regression model, or sophisticated, such as Deep Reinforcement Learning with Double Q-Learning (if you're interested in some light reading, there are articles written on the impact of the original Deep Reinforced Learning overestimating, hence the need for some modification). We plan to tackle the subject of AI in-depth in the future.

ADOPTERS—EARLY AND RESISTANT

RPA has already been adopted large scale. Fortune 500 Companies and large-scale organizations have at least started investing in these technologies if they are not using them across multiple departments. If you're waiting for me to tell you 'the early bird gets the worm,' keep waiting. We are going to look at the pros and cons of early adoption of technology and resistance to adopting new technologies.

Adopting RPA, or any technology, for that matter, can be a detriment if it's done incorrectly. As a consultant, I look at both sides of the proverbial coin. The cons will be interspersed with the adoption process, as we move through the information. Ultimately, the worst problem that could be encountered is not assessing the needs and capabilities of the chosen programs correctly. Buying unnecessary programs that utilize resources for training and integration creates chaos and may cause businesses to shy away from future growth. Without a doubt, dealing with the frustration of implementing wrong technology in the workplace would cause cold feet but it can be the difference between growth and stagnation or existence and failure, depending on the business and brand involved. If you have been down the wrong path, hire a reputable consultant to help in the process.

Why do people adopt RPA? Initially, RPA is adopted for cost reduction-through automated processes and a reduction in payroll hours for mundane tasks. The second benefit is to increase data capture, creating audit checkpoints of what happened, which inherently reduces litigation. Human error is significantly reduced when clients or customers are filling in their personal information fields and the RPA is capturing their agreement to different contracts or disclaimers and storing it in easily accessible files. The RPA is also able to flag missing fields for human follow-up, so there are multiple checkpoints forming a streamlined process that makes interactions with companies more predictable and uninterrupted from one client to another, reducing the stress of reviewed interactions with a turnover staff. The simple rule-based tasks RPA handles would-be entry-level jobs requiring constant training which adds stress to retaining employees and customers.

A tertiary benefit to adopting RPA is increasing revenue by having greater customer outreach. With a more accessible approach to customer acquisition, more customers can be served, and orders processed. This is where we see a con to RPA rear its head. If adoption is unsuccessful or incomplete, problems will arise. If your competitors are successfully using RPA, they will gain more revenue which translates to their growth in product/service development and increased marketing while you are still handling things at a slower pace. While a company can survive competition, and it is a healthy part of commerce, there is product and company loyalty that can affect your customer acquisition while catching up to the competition.

There are people who adopt early and fail. RPA will not take a bad business model and magically transform it into something successful. Bad business practices or subpar products/services cannot be transformed by successful RPA. Starting the right business at the right time or business in the wrong market can happen. RPA isn't the downfall or the sole reason for success, that isn't the message of this book.

People who implement RPA and fail sometimes stop attempting to adapt technologically. These people will be worse off than if they never tried. It's important to learn from failures. Some people start, stop, and call it a failure before the RPA was put into operation. Some people hire the wrong firm to get them started and they pay $200 Million dollars for one robot, expecting an extreme digital transformation to find that their expectation won't be actualized without much more money dumped into the project, making recouping the investment almost impossible.

There's a right way to perform a digital transformation and doing the research helps ensure more possibility of a successful mission into technology driven advances. The right way to do it is to evaluate the current processes and paint the picture. If you need help doing that, get help by bringing people in. The wrong way to do it is to hand the keys to your business to someone who doesn't know your business, right?

Business and government have different goals, and both benefit greatly from RPA. Government adopts RPA to increase the happiness of constituents. Reducing the frustration of constituents at the local, state, and federal level by using RPA to handle influx of requests can improve quality of life in areas. Let's use the example of the DMV (paying fines and standing in line to pay for things like tags and registration fees). People don't like spending hours in line waiting for things like this. They want to get in, get out, and get on with their day. When they have to use government services, increasing their satisfaction with the experience with the government workers is key. This can help with re-election for elected officials.

We will cover the automation of processes more specifically later, which might help in fashioning a plan that works for different companies, organizations, government entities, etc. As RPA possibilities and applications are explained, you will be able to start painting the picture for your organization or company.

THE TECHNICAL SIDE

Remember the famous blockchain phase (fad)? As it started to spin up as an emerging technology, not too long ago, people were scratching their heads trying to grasp how the various pop-up blockchains worked. One of my colleagues worked on a white paper with a blockchain technology, early on, and when she explained to the creators that she wasn't any help because she couldn't comprehend the way it worked. She had a list of logical questions so she could help edit the paper for clarity and so the readers could understand. Instead of answering her questions, their response to her was, "If you understood, we wouldn't trust you." Stymied, she recused herself from the project and walked away without getting paid.

Other technology trends have had an incredible impact: The PC, the emergence of social media. We will unveil the biggest technological advances at the end of this chapter, then rank them in importance. Will RPA be another blockchain or will it have an irreversible effect and change on our working lives? Blockchain is making an obvious comeback with the surge in crypto currency and NFT. Perhaps it will a greater sticking power now.

The statistics suggest it will change jobs—what jobs are available, what jobs get digitized, and what careers disappear as an option. Gartner cited in 2018, RPA was the fastest growing software at a 68% clip.[1] According to Deloitte, RPA will reach near global adoption by 2023.[2] More recently, in 2017, Deloitte shared HFS Research expectations that RPA services and products would reach $433 million with an expected increase to $1.2 billion by 2021.[3] These surveys and general discussion in the industry, along with our own partner ecosystem success, would indicate that this trend does indeed seem to be expanding and that RPA will be a global force, which is why understanding the digital worker is important.

So, the real question is: What will the impact be on everyone from business, to government, to you and me? If we think about some of the most recent historical inventions, such as the touch screen (which permeates the everyday life of every individual), will RPA have that reach?

Based on the Deloitte survey, with a 12-month ROI (return on investment), it seems certain that businesses will near universally adopt RPA. It is true that many take the approach of seeing what one bot can do first and pause while they figure out how to react to the changes made in the workplace. This will cause some tool churn in the industry, but the software and concept will continue on. Let's dive into ROI a little further. Return on investment (ROI) for RPA can have multiple tiers, here are a few that are widely recognized in the industry.

ROI Analysis is conducted when creating a business case for RPA implementation and is performed to arrive at CBA (cost-benefit analysis):

a) Total Savings includes:

1) How much manual time and effort will be saved with the automation deployed.

2) Is the output quality improved? How many errors are reduced in the process? Align cost per error to derive savings.

3) How much is the increase in the overall gain in productivity?

4) How much is the percentage increased in customer satisfaction and brand awareness?

5) Is Business agility being improved?

6) Improved regulatory compliance and data governance.

b) Total Investment includes RPA software procurement cost annually + Annual Maintenance + Experts training and or implementation cost + IT infra cost + IT software cost [e.g.: process mining software, Visio, any third-party software required]
== Add the above savings [a] for one year and deduct the Investment cost [b] for RPA implementation for a year to arrive at ROI.

If there wasn't a return on investment, RPA wouldn't be effective. While there is an obvious monetary return on investment, there are other ROIs that aren't as tangible as receipts and ledgers. The rest of the ROI story can be told in employee satisfaction: Employees that were stuck with mundane tasks are now able to focus on more fulfilling projects and instead of taking sick days or quitting, causing training costs to go up, the retention rate can improve. ROI may be the program finding accounting anomalies that help catch embezzling much faster than if someone is waiting on a paper ledger from banks and credit cards and is just looking at amounts because they are only responsible for the bottom line and are expected to get so many tasks per day done so things slip unnoticed while they try to juggle multiple tasks. The RPA can be set to catch what a quick once over might miss at first glance. RPA can also catch patterns and flag the information for further review. Reports on overtime/payroll/ and expenses, profit/losses, accounts payable and receivable, etc. can be generated more regularly and sent to key decision makers. The opportunities and options can be broad or limited, based on the specific needs of each organization.

TECH ADVANCEMENTS THAT SHOOK THE WORLD

If we are to make an observation about the IT trends that will go down in history, we can easily see the forerunners have a common theme: They changed working lives while entering our personal lives too. Let's look at the past 20-plus years of IT trends that have been brought to boardroom attention. Some were IT trends; some were hype, and some were real. The impact technology has on our lives is undeniable.

The Infamous Y2K: The turning of the century was uncertain in the tech world. Mainstream media was creating panic by telling people that the computers were not ready for the millennial turnover, and that at midnight January 1, 2000, the computers would forget they were computers and crash because they didn't exist in 1900. Of course, that wasn't the full picture or explanation, but it set people to prepping by filling their homes with supplies, expecting electrical grids and n=banking to go down for as long as it took the tech world to reassure the computers that it was okay to come out and play in 2000, not 1900. Those of us who worked in technology firms can remember the endless meetings, the contingency planning (I would suggest Year 2000 planning did change disaster recovery planning majorly), the holiday bans, the worry was all for nothing. There was no disaster of epic proportions. Certain programs had to be recoded, but it wasn't going to be an epic failure, even if we missed the midnight deadline, because information was backed up and stored for recovery.

The Dot.com Boom and the Emergence of Commercial Internet: For the older generations, we remember a time when computers and smart devices didn't dominate every moment of the day. Millennials, and the generations after them, will learn about a world not connected electronically, like they do now about a world before cars or without electricity. Some point to the Amish as the example of antiquated living compared to our lives of connectivity and instant access to all information at our fingertips that is the norm now. There were business applications, internet searching, but extraordinarily little purchasing online towards the beginning. Adaptation and adoption of the Internet was fairly slow at the beginning. Our lives have been changed beyond recognition by the internet. Our working lives have moved from file folders in huge filing rooms in offices to flash drives and email. Can you remember working in an office pre-internet? I can, and it was indescribably different. Every aspect of life has changed: The way we communicate, the

way we shop, the way we're entertained, the way we eat, what we do, where we go, how we get there.
The interesting point here, coming back to the dot.com boom, there was an explosion and a subsequent market correction. The benefit in hindsight was just part of the journey, a correction.

The Dot.com Boom led to the Dot.com Bust. Money stopped being poured into things with relatively little value—Remember the Hotmail handouts to connect to the internet being handed out at checkouts? Internet service providers changed, venture capital got held back, and companies going public had to show viability in the market. A lot of monetizing wasn't ready for how quickly internet usage was about to change the technological landscape. Some things made big money but fizzled out while other things slowly and steadily adapted and grew.

Big Data, Data Lakes, Data in General: Data became an issue as a result of our connectivity and subsequent increased use of systems. Data was a result of change, not a cause. Yes, some of the data 'revolutions' changed our IT infrastructures. Suddenly, we didn't have to guess at the competitor's sales and locating all relevant competitors in any given market. Now, we just had to sift through and file the data available. Research in many fields was digitized and made available for consumers, which was also utilized by other fields, advancing knowledge at incredible rates. Data wasn't a problem when written, the problem was access. If data is incomplete, erroneous, intentionally corrupted, or any other variation of wrong, the interconnectivity of bad data can cause a plethora of issues. This is where RPA can thrive or tank. RPA can be set to catch data sets and help locate corrupted data. Depending on how the information is connected, RPA could fix or flag data within an organization to bring attention to the issue. The wholeness of information and the transformation of data is inherent to the application of all programming, and it is vital that data structures are maintained and retained.

Analytics: Analytics are also a consequence of data. We have to be able to make sense of this mammoth dump of stuff. A consequence of change, not a cause. Not to minimize the catastrophic problems with Covid-19, but to make a relevant point: Analytical data in business can make all the difference. As sales of toilet paper spiked during the early shutdown phase of the pandemic, great analytical data between the inventories of all the stores and the toilet paper manufacturers could have given accurate analytical details to the various manufacturers to kick production into turbo gear sooner to meet the demand of frenzied shoppers worried about running out of TP. Using great analytics helps determine how to react and make changes to organizational behavior. Now, imagine these same companies take the same number of months to correct their high gear manufacturing of toilet paper. They will need new warehouses for the fluffy white stuff and may have to readjust their workforce, possibly laying off several employees, which could cause long-term harm to both employees and the manufacturers.

The iPhone or the Touch Screen Phone: Steve Jobs will be studied and his impact on the world brought technology to the masses: Everybody developed a relationship with technology as a result of the touchscreen. However, this change was to our personal lives. The flip phone was an improvement to the cordless home phone. This marvel folded up and could ring from your pocket. We will politely leave the glorified garage door opener (the Beeper) kindly out of this discussion. The flip phone made way for the Blackberry, which had a keyboard that took up half the phone, advancing from the multiple keying of the numbers to reach the letters necessary to make the words to send texts. The interaction with the device was increasing. Enter the touch screen. Real estate on the phone increased and all the sudden, the phone became a recording device, camera, video camera, TV, menu, computer, etc.

Networked Devices: Routers are the glue that keeps everyone connected. While routers take a backseat, they are foundational and not to be underestimated in importance. Wi-Fi doesn't work on its own. It requires a line connection to a router. The difference between analog versus digital, there is no more dial-up. This is a cart before the horse debate, or which came first—chicken or the egg. It was the router; it just isn't as exciting as the other tech topics.

Social Media: The way social media has changed so many landscapes is vast, it will be a chore to keep this short. We live in a world of influencers now. People get paid on social media to promote products and companies. Social media has created more jobs than it gets credit for, but that's just a bonus. Social media gives a larger voice to a smaller subset of people. For instance, micro loans go to farmers in Africa because social media has been able to get some of the micro loan success stories out to people that want to help others. Social media has changed how businesses reach and interact with their customer base. Fifty years ago, Walter Cronkite was the largest influencer, now many more people get to participate on swaying public perception one way or another.

This becomes dangerous with the cancel culture we are currently seeing. Just like one awesome viral video can launch a small business, one cancel culture post could take down a big company. The technology landscape changes with social culture, with both information and misinformation starting an equation that has a sliding scale towards the future success of businesses. Social media has also helped many start home businesses or join MLM (multi-level marketing) business options.

RANKING

Everybody loves a list. Let's create one. In order of impact:

1. RPA will be shaping the future. Obviously, I see more than I have conveyed to this point (it is only chapter 2. RPA is the steppingstone to where we are going, one of the building blocks to the future. Henry Ford invented the production line, which enhanced and revolutionized manufacturing. Robots have taken over man in Henry Ford's production line,

creating the rivets, bending the material into a car on the line. RPA will lead us into expanding AI.

3. The Touch Screen helped evolve and revolutionize how we interacted with our technology. The horizon has more interesting innovation: Oculus, implants that make the computers and human beings' merge. These advances are exciting to some and terrifying to others.

4. Social Media will go through many more changes, like it has since Myspace and Early Facebook. LinkedIn may not always be the top business networking platform. It will be interesting to see what happens with TikTok, Snapchat, Twitter, Instagram, Pinterest, and the newcomers trying to gain users. If the options for social media don't prove that needs are changing to include online networking options that meet the desires of different groups of people, there might be nothing else to prove it for you. In a world of increased network connectivity, backyard and in-person connections are failing to serve people. Many don't even know their immediate neighbors but are connected to people around the world.

5. Big data makes more about literally everything available. That's a huge deal. Without data, the next point on our lost wouldn't be here:

6. Analytics. Analytics helps track the data, even who might visit a website, where on the site the visitor spent the most time, whether they are part of the conversion rate to a marketing campaign, etc.

7. Y2K is inconsequential in the future. It is just an interesting reminder of the ways that computers and AI are a part of our lives. It's a good

reminder, when we think about it, of how digitized the world has truly become.

Please note, this was not a comprehensive list of what impacts the technology world. Just a handful of things that unite the collective memories of most readers, and the topics that are important to weigh in on this discussion.

EVOLUTION TO REVOLUTION

The technological revolution of the workplace has been happening and people adapt. Hearing about future changes doesn't always foster confidence in the ability to adopt the changes, but we can look at advances in history to remind us all how positive and normal changes are to life.

There are horse-and-buggy people that didn't adapt to the upcoming Ford Model A. They figured that most people would opt for the old way. Their business was making wheels, building and repairing buggies, forming and placing horseshoes, breeding and training horses for buggies. Business was booming, so they didn't see the car as a threat to their industry. There were people that saw themselves as part of the transportation industry which meant they were committed to all forms of transportation, so when they saw the emerging car, they weren't threatened by it, but sought to figure out what would be needed to work on this advancing transportation model. The car would need tires, repairs, fluids for the motors, fuel, cleaning, etc.

Racing cars would emerge and delivery systems using the cars.

The difference between the horse-and-buggy people and the transportation industry people was vision and innovation. Where are you in your industry? Is your vision too streamlined, keeping your company from growth?

The transportation industry didn't quit evolving with the car. Airplanes, boats, trains, and the automobiles have led to space exploration and rockets. There are transportation toys and government jobs. Transportation as an industry has created numerous jobs in design, innovation, manufacturing, sales, road/rail repair, vehicle repair, fuel lines from field work to refinery, rubber work, steel work, the list can go on. That is micro (one vehicle) versus industry (the big picture). Now imagine, you are the horse-and-buggy person who misses the transportation industry opportunities and goes out of business when the horse-and-buggy goes the way horse-and-buggies went. Obviously, there are still the Amish, but they are a self-contained community, not a huge market for horse-and-buggy people.

The radio shows gave way to television series and the big screen. Typewriters moved over to make room for computers. Computers evolved until they are faster and store more information than ever. Now, we give them more responsibility. It's evolution.

What is eliminated for the advances that are coming? We will cover it more in depth later, but entire career choices will be eliminated. The task-oriented jobs will be taken over by RPA, so the people holding task-oriented jobs will have to learn and adapt or go somewhere else.

The Industrial Revolution shows how fast things can change. Steam to locomotive. Buggy to car. Propeller to jet engine. RPA will revolutionize the workplace, while RPA evolves. RPA will help companies transition from repetitive processes being an employee's task to the Digital Worker conducting activities expeditiously and off hours. This means reports can be available when key workers show up in the morning, instead of waiting on reports during the same hours an entry level employee is creating the data. Margins of error narrow making efficiency more guaranteed. Turnover keeps many companies spending resources on training and retraining entry level employees to manage simple tasks. The long-term investment that could have saved countless hours and loads of money, would have been better used transitioning from people being responsible for thirty-plus tasks to automating to increase productivity. This takes high performers from basic tasks to focusing on the growth of projects that advance entire departments, companies, and cities to the next level. What that looks like depends on the type of entity using RPA, but the applications are endless.

Chapter 3

Where Is RPA Now?

ROBOTIC DESKTOP AUTOMATION

What is it? Robotic Desktop Automation (RDA) is the automation of specific processes, or parts of a process, using an attended bot. You have certain processes you go through in your working day, each one taking a certain amount of your time and attention. RDA allows you to replace one or more of these manual processes with an automated process that you initiate.

As an example: Prioritizing Email. You might arrive at work in the morning and want to have your high priority emails identified. In my case, I'll go into my email, and I'll look for emails from customers; then, I'll look for emails from certain people in my organization; finally, I'll look at vendor emails.

The RDA approach would be to create a bot

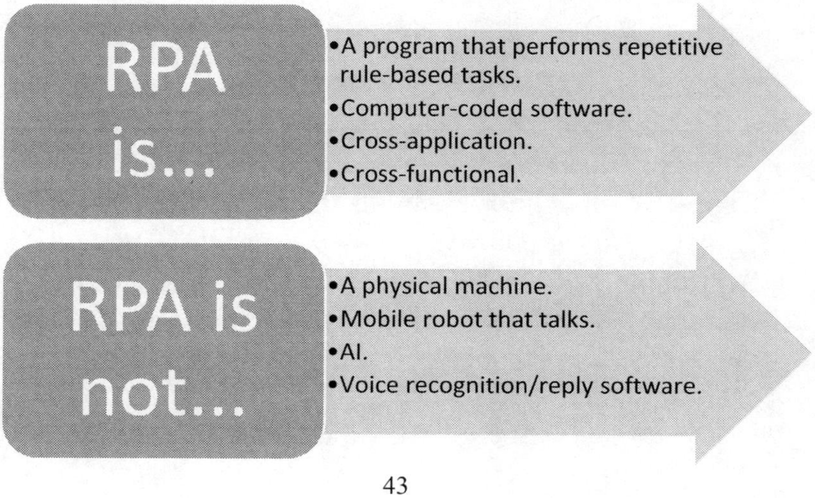

that will process your incoming email. That bot will categorize and prioritize your emails, based on what you typically do. Now, rather than having to process your email manually, you click the button that initiates the bot. Once it's completed its task, you get a message to tell you that your emails have been prioritized, and you can go ahead and look at them.

WHAT RPA CAN DO:

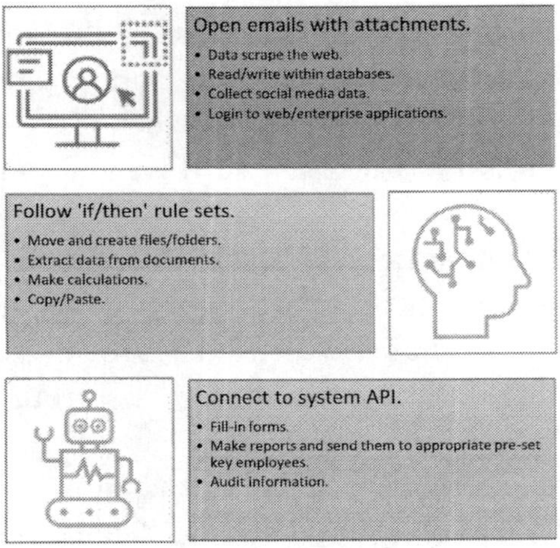

ATTENDED BOTS

Attended bots require the user to start the process. There may be a start or run option. The Digital Worker interacts with the human. There will be validation scenarios, desktop scenarios, meaning the human worker will validate reports. For instance, there may be a data set that needs to be translated to an Excel Spreadsheet. The Digital Worker can extract the numbers, put it into the Spreadsheet, and the human will take over applying the information where it is needed. Before, the human may have needed to copy then paste all of the data line by line, which is time consuming and one mistake could offset the entire Spreadsheet, taking hours to find the mistake before painstakingly fixing the rest just to get to the point an attended Digital Worker could have gotten to quickly. RDA is always attended. We will cover unattended bots with RPA.

What are the benefits? In general, the benefits of RDA are realized in two main ways:

- Reduced time spent on routine tasks. Rather than spending time trawling through emails and identifying the important messages, I can move straight to dealing with them.

- Reduced rate of human error. I might have a hundred or more emails in my inbox, and could perhaps miss an important one, whereas the computer will reliably follow the rules I give it and identify all the important emails.

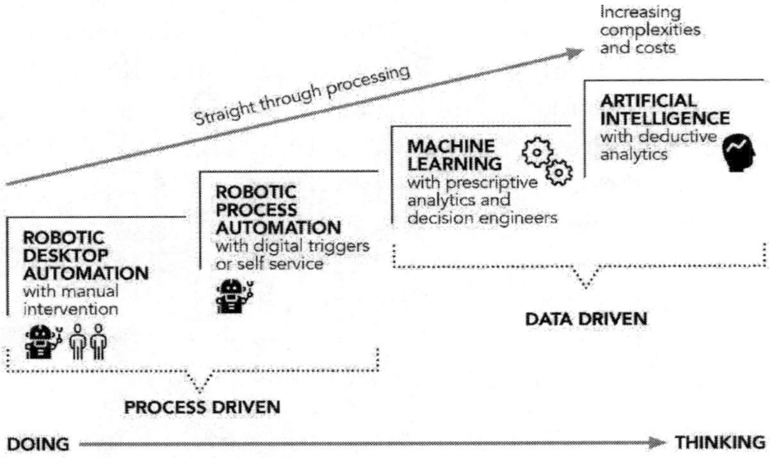

ROBOTIC PROCESS AUTOMATION

What is it? Robotic Process Automation (RPA) is the mimicking of human behavior for processes that require no true cognitive thought. In other words, the automated bot replicates a series of routine steps that a human operator would undertake. Furthermore, it replicates those steps without any human intervention: Rather than a human operator clicking a button to initiate the bot, the initiation happens automatically, at a scheduled time.

RPA is sometimes described as "swivel-chair integration;" this refers to the way that a typical process to be automated will involve a human operator needing to move information between two or more unconnected systems.

UNATTENDED BOTS

Unattended bots will emulate the behavior of a human and can be scheduled to run without human interaction. For instance, in a situation where payroll must be calculated at week's end, the unattended bot can be set to run at midnight on the last day, calculating hourly, salaried, and commissioned employee payroll using the rules set forth. As long as all time off, vacation days, etc. were entered correctly into the system, the report could be ready for the accounting department bright and early in the morning, instead of someone coming in and needing to manually calculate all employee's pay.

What are the benefits? In general, much like RDA, the benefits of RPA are realized in two main ways:

- Reduced time spent on routine tasks: Rather than spending a lot of time on mundane tasks, such as checking the contents of one report against the contents of another, the commissions analyst can spend her time on more cognitively demanding tasks, such as investigating errors.
- Reduced rate of human error: The automated bot is well suited to tasks such as comparing long lists of transactions to one another, looking for discrepancies. Human operators are poorly suited for tasks of that type, since they get tired, lose concentration, and easily miss the very things they're looking for in lengthy files.

An example: Ensuring Compliance with Equal Pay Legislation. A major issue in Europe right now is equal pay. Whether you're a man or a woman, if you have the same title and the same levels of experience and qualification, the law says that you should be paid the same. How do you enforce that? How do you make sure that that's actually what happens in your business?

Logically, you have to create a report that says: "Based on the following criteria, here are my salary bands, and this is the level of variation that's acceptable, perhaps plus-minus 3% or plus-minus 5%. For anybody who falls outside that acceptable variation, you must take corrective action."

The challenge comes when you start looking at the detail of determining that two people are in the same role and should therefore receive equal pay. Is it based on length of service? Is it based on job title? Is it based on location? Is it based on qualifications and educational measures (certifications, licenses, degrees, etc.)? Much of the relevant information is likely to be found in performance reviews, résumés, and other information sources that have typically been stored in a Word document format, Excel spreadsheet format, or some other format that isn't easily accessible.

Using RPA, a bot can be created that will interrogate all these disparate sources and load the relevant information into an accessible data structure. That information then allows you to answer the key question: are we complying with equal pay legislation? RPA will analyze the criteria dataset and create a list of information that needs human attention. The ability of RPA stops at the ruleset. It can only flag for attention what is outside of the parameters that are set.

Suggestions will be applied when data needs human interaction. It will ask, "What do you want to do?" If set up within acceptable parameters, the RPA may show you the rule set. Let's say there is a female sales rep that makes a base pay of $80,000 plus 10% commission. There are also three male sales reps that started twenty years ago and make a base-pay of $145,000 plus the 10% bonus but have higher quotas and sell more. The rule base, following the law, may require the same quota which may mean that the base pay should be equal. What is a company to do?

The ethical problem isn't RPA's issue. RPA just points out the disparity, and the company will have to make decisions based on the law. The hard and fast rule might be to hand the men walking papers and make them eligible for rehire. They are used to higher quotas so may make more money based on their experience or the company may be able to justify the disparity.

THE DIGITAL WORKER VERSUS HUMANS

To talk about where RPA stands currently within the workforce, we have to look at the capabilities of the machine. Page load time will still be the page load time, whether the digital worker or a human is running the applications. The Digital Worker isn't going to change the speed of the computer, although the systems can be updated and modified to maximize for different variables that will enhance work computers – for both the Digital Worker and the human.

There are clear implications for all sectors that make the Digital Worker invaluable as an asset to the human workers: Expediency of information AND accuracy and thoroughness of information and data. The Digital Worker can deliver faster and with less mistakes.

Humans make errors when transferring data. Imagine someone transferring a huge spreadsheet into different systems that require checks and balances, but they mix up a few lines and all transferred data is corrupted. The human would never intentionally make this large of a mistake, especially when they are most likely the one that has to start over on the task. Now, imagine that there is a deadline and opportunities or vital processes within the company hinge upon these reports and entries. This is more than errors when up against the grain, now, it's a catastrophe. Humans make mistakes, but bots make less mistakes. The mistakes bots make are based on human error—if a field entry is incorrect, a bot will transfer the information present in the field. As long as the Digital Worker is following a rule-based function, the mistakes encountered will be linked to human error.

Removing the monotonous copy-paste nature of mundane tasks by assigning the repetitive work to the Digital Worker frees up the human capital (time) for clients, customers, constituents, and other projects that need more hands on. The benefits to morale for the human are numerous; now the human isn't stuck navigating between pages but is instead managing anything flagged by the Digital Worker and the human gets to spend more of their day doing more meaningful work.

The Digital Worker will not increase the time it takes to accomplish a task. Whether the time savings is substantial or not may depend on the task. Will an industry leader value the Digital Worker for making an hour task into a five-minute task? That fifty-five-minute time savings may not seem like much overall, especially if it's a task that must only be done a handful of times in any given month. The value is that a mistake could cost more in the long run.

LEGACY SYSTEMS

Using RPA to handle interactions between legacy systems to create digital process flows is a great use for RPA. The low-hanging fruit for RPA is in connecting and smoothing over processes involving older systems. RPA can automate them at UI level, extending their useful lifespan and effectiveness by "patching up" the gaps in existing processes with bot activities. This mainframe or "legacy system" is mission critical to the organization but not friendly with new technology. Can you imagine the differences between notepad and the current Word software—night and day. RPA gives companies the chance to keep notepad legacy systems that can talk to current programs and extend the life of the legacy system for the company. For business leaders and IT heads, this is a great way to overcome issues with older systems and get more value from them. It's particularly easy to make the business case when it defers major systems investment.

Legacy systems that don't effectively integrate with newer technology tend to demand a lot of manual intervention, so there's also an excellent time saving, and efficiency gain in automating multi-stage human-system interactions that can be both tortuous and error-prone.

Without a doubt, this is an excellent use case for RPA and a good way to demonstrate how it can work to deliver immediate benefit. But it can under-deliver in some instances due to the lack of bot flexibility. For example, minor changes to a front-end user interface (UI) are easily absorbed by a human operator. But RPA bots require precise instruction to carry out a chain of actions in a consistent environment, even a tiny change to a UI or a security update can halt an RPA operation.

Of course, with good RPA management practices, IT teams can maintain systems appropriately and update the RPA to ensure continuous, effective operation. But it does require ongoing attention: an RPA bot cannot adapt by itself to seemingly trivial changes in the same way that a human can. We have seen some RPA deployments abandoned because expectations were over-set, and it was seen as a one-time fix. Digital Workers are not genies, they require maintenance and care to keep advancing with your organization.

AUTOMATE INTERACTIONS WITH NEW APPS

The second most common application of RPA is in connecting newer applications, where it's possible to automate at the API level. Technically, this is a more resilient approach. Because of the nature of API architecture, bots that interact at this level are able to accommodate some minor variations at UI level without management intervention.

Organizations that are using RPA in this way can drive more strategic value from it, even though the immediate pain relief, payback or freeing up of operational resources may not be as impactful. Rather than creating a workaround, IT teams are building RPA into their operational and development plans, to improve the productivity and efficiency of processes that are working effectively but sub-optimally, rather than dramatically fixing something that's broken or on the brink of collapse.

Using RPA to optimize newer applications is a more robust approach to existing systems that have a reasonable shelf life. It's a way to harness the power of RPA as business as usual, looking for opportunities to apply it to current infrastructure throughout the business.

Even though the savings are low now, automating intervention with new apps is a great way to keep your IT team and coders working towards the optimal Center of Excellence for the company. While each new application may not have immediate benefits from automation, down the line that minor tie in might have major implications.

BOT ONLY WORK

Designing and redesigning processes specifically to be managed by bots is possible. This is the most forward-looking and strategic approach to RPA, adopted by industry and sector leaders who have a clear and realistic understanding of what RPA can deliver.

These organizations are building robotic automation into all future infrastructure, process planning and system development. They are exploring the potential to augment RPA with artificial intelligence (AI) to be more self-sufficient, creating machine learning that can continually review and enhance processes. This will be the future. AI will continue to grow and be effective with RPA.

In our view, all successful organizations need to be developing in the middle of all this—tie in legacy systems, the most important new applications, and be willing to move forward with more processes as they become available. Deploying RPA strategically in this way requires experience, confidence, sector and operational understanding as well as strong technical expertise in robotics.

The early headline benefit of RPA may be to patch up creaking systems to make short term efficiency gains, but this can't continue indefinitely. For any organization that has more than a tactical IT support department, the future IT and digital vision and strategy needs to include RPA intrinsically. At a minimum, organizations must make RPA efficiencies integral to their ongoing systems development plan, as a priority for investment in new technology.

Chapter 4

RPA, AI, and the CEO

An interesting question entering the world of technology is: Will AI replace the CEO role? The follow-up question is: What decisions can be made more intelligently by a machine based on data?

TRADITIONAL VERSUS NONTRADITIONAL TASKS

Traditional tasks that artificial intelligence could take on and make small work of would fall in line with undertakings that are led by data sets that must be interpreted: forecasts based on current information (real time data or regular reports); directionally check on assets (human capital based-checking schedules, sales performance, etc.); year over year projections (intelligence engine); production commands and reporting; education; sales distribution; human capital data reporting (how many employees at specific locations with specific skillsets and their corresponding performance reports); using historical data in the market to promote suggestions. That is a lot of busy work that could be tracked more efficiently with AI and suggestions could become more available than if a human had to access and read multiple reports and research before forming teams or opinions based on their own understanding of the data.

The nontraditional duties cannot be done by AI, not et or in the immediate future, and still needs human logic and hands on attention. A human can choose an entirely new trajectory for the company based on market trends that are emerging independently of historical data. Businesses need CEOs to give guidance in areas with no prior data, and the great news continues to be that companies want to innovate and grow into spaces that can be dreamt up within the framework of the company's vision. Having AI handle the data thick information to spit out suggestions that free up a creative CEO to grow the company to new heights should be exciting to any company that wants longevity in changing markets.

Machine learning is based on information, following factors, and can greatly impact the top and bottom line. AI could be great predicting forecasts for a product, especially since it can pull data sets for similar products from many more sources than a person may be able to find in a timely fashion. The data AI could build might show markets that the proposed product would thrive in. AI would then take the external information and make decisions for marketing campaigns based on demand trends. Machine learning handling intrinsic and extrinsic data while marking a profit share increase isn't to be frowned upon.

BACK TO THE QUESTION-TO CEO OR NOT TO CEO?

Again, businesses will always need humans. BUT...Will the way that humans interact within the company change? All publicly traded companies are required to have a board of directors. The board of directors is in charge of hiring and firing, dividend payouts and policies, and executive compensation. Legally, a corporation isn't required to have a CEO. It's the traditional way things are done, but if we are changing the norms in business, it is conceivable that the dynamics for shareholders could change.

The consolidation of data could allow a board of directors to cut back on C-level title holders and their large compensation plans while using the algorithms to make decisions. AI could look at projected sales and examine options to increase profit margins based on historical data. The reason humans must be involved could look something like this: 97% of a viewer base of a news corporation is white. AI would look at this data, the customers' behaviors, their interaction with the content online and determine which articles were most popular, formulating the way that the customers prefer their news written. AI would determine a hiring pattern that would go against laws from 1964 on not discriminating in the hiring process. AI's choice based on available information and data would cost the corporation more because AI using the consumer base to make hiring decisions based on race instead of talent and ability would be a horrible practice. Having diversity within our companies is important for many reasons. There are entire books and seminars on this, so I won't expound here, we are only covering the intricacies of decisions machine learning could cause if left unchecked.

There are nefarious issues that could arise with AI unchallenged at the helm. Imagine an oil and gas company that puts AI in charge. AI looks at the closest competitor's pipeline and decides it needs to beat out the competitor. The natural way of competition looks at price and quality, if both are comparable, there needs to be another strategy. AI might decide a take down of servers or hijacking them could give the home company competitive advantage. This might take a competitor a few months to fix, while the home company positions itself as the local provider. Now, imagine AI run industries where the computers have figured out that taking out other computers is a successful way to cripple competition. There is nothing good about that scenario, but if we can conceive it, and AI is smarter than a human, it could be a real scenario pretty quick, left unchecked.

Even though technology advancement is my business, it must be noted that we can't and won't get rid of humans with machines, even if the scenario is talked about on stages to audiences. Humans know not to create situations that aren't optimal to other humans and life.

RPA is the way to get the company optimized for CEOs to advance their teams and companies to new heights. RPA isn't confined to helping companies. Coming up, we will explore how education, government, the medical realm, and other industries can utilize RPA to maximize their efforts.

OPERATING RPA IN THE BUSINESS SETTING

RPA in business is an in-depth conversation. Let's boil it down before going into the specifics: Using Digital Workers to maximize human capital creates cost benefits and opportunities for growth. Not all types of organizations use the same processes and programs, yet all organizations can optimize their processes with RPA. This is where Lanshore or other experts in the field are vital to making sure that available resources put towards new technologies is utilized correctly.

The private sector is known for being able to offer more money for tedious jobs and mind numbingly boring tasks (as compared to government jobs, which we cover later). When the repetitive tasks get eliminated by RPA taking them over, employees start engaging in the projects that matter. Job satisfaction is greatly increased when Digital Workers are employed.

There are four main areas affected by RPA adoption within organizations. Employee satisfaction with their work increases. This stalls massive turnover rates and training costs associated with the hiring process and high turnover. Customer/client satisfaction is boosted due to employees being more available to tend to the customer/client needs. Without deadlines on copy/paste projects or preparation of numerous reports, human capital is focused on the most important growth factor for organizations: maintaining, growing, and seeking out new customers and clients. Risk management becomes more streamlined and assessable. The Digital Worker can be coded to watch the margins for anomalies that can alert organizations in live time to issues and opportunities. Digital Workers increase productivity, all the way around. The savings Digital Workers provide is real, not just soft savings.

Building a company on the forefront of digital transformation doesn't have to be daunting or impossible. While the intricacies of how RPA works may dilute the importance of the Digital Worker, we are committed to making the transformation successful and sustainable for the best possible outcome.

ADOPTING RPA

Adopting new technologies has its hurdles. The hush-hush side of early adoption of technology is it can be detrimental if done wrong. We shouldn't be afraid to discuss these things.

Advantages of adopting RPA early are initially:

1. Cost reduction
2. Increase data capture
3. Increase revenue

When the global corporate world is competing for clients, customers, and contracts, companies can end up behind their competitors quicker and faster. The catch is: with the right tools, better customer service, and higher rates of good reviews that come from customer satisfaction, success stories also abound. RPA is a tool to the top, but not the guarantee of a certain magnitude of success.

What can go wrong? Early adopters can fail at implementation. Imagine getting in a sports car parked in front of a building. This thing is made for speed, made to take curves. You floor it. Straight into the building and don't even attempt to hit the brakes. You are going to go somewhere, but for a drive on an open road isn't one of the places you're going. People do it all the time with technology. You don't blame the toaster when you leave it in the box, "Oh, my toast didn't prepare toast." You would recognize that user error and neglect caused the toast to not be ready. With technology, there is user preparation and correct setup involved. You might have to read user manuals if you are preparing RPA yourself or have the tech team train the users.

People who don't stop and learn from failure are worse off than the people that never try to implement new technology. People that keep using technology wrong to then have an excuse for failure would have been better off without new technology. No one blames the ballpoint pen for a misspelled word, the Digital Worker is no different. If the processes aren't coded into the design, the Digital Worker will run the rule-based operations and nothing else.

The right way to approach automation is by evaluating the processes that are in use already within an organization then automate what is cost efficient and frees up the most human capital. The absolute wrong way to go about implementing new technology is to hand the keys to someone who doesn't know the business or tech options at all. If figuring it all out is outside your wheelhouse, or you would rather hire a team that knows what they are doing, see the 'Why Lanshore?' chapter.

IDENTIFYING MISSING PROCESSES

After figuring out the different processes in action within an organization, there may be missing processes that must be accounted for to make the Digital Worker run efficiently. For instance, say the company decides that automating payroll and banking information with an accounting program, like QuickBooks, is where they want to start with RPA, and the login and password phases aren't coded into the program. The Digital Worker cannot bypass prompts a human must complete. That is a simple example, but it goes on from there. If the percentages for employees' compensation or their salary/hourly wages aren't in the system correctly, the Digital Worker won't be able to complete payroll or logging all pertinent information in the correct places. Human error creates technological errors.

IDENTIFYING REDUNDANT PROCESSES

Redundant processes usually come up when companies generate reports as the outcome of a process. A lot of what they're doing is information management and information sharing. This is the equivalent of the famous TPS Report in the movie *Office Space*. So, we would look at it and ask, "Okay, why are you generating this report? Who's consuming it? What are they consuming here?" The answer might come back, "Well, we've always done it. We've done it for the last 30 years." Often they'll say, "Well, let's just shut it off and see who complains. Then we'll find out whether anybody is using this."

The same thing goes for processes. What happens if we shut this process off? What happens if we don't do this step? What happens if we rebuild this step to be something more meaningful? The reason for RPA is not just making better use of employees' time, but expediency. If something takes three hours, I want it to take three minutes.

THE HIGH COGNITION FUTURE

Current jobs still include the kind of spreadsheet creation where it's click, copy, and paste. RPA is removing that kind of low cognition task. Instead, employees will be asked what's the real business impetus of what they're doing. Are they helping customers and clients find new ways to interact with products and services? Are they creating new opportunities and building healthy business relationships that propel future business interactions through partnerships and rapport?

Managers will be talking to workers and saying, "I'm not going to fire you, but you need to provide something of value in your thought process." That's where the future of jobs is heading—innovation. Mundane office tasks will be automated, so more fulfilling work can take center stage. What we can't yet automate is the ability to think ahead and plan the future of core business.

If a sales company thinks about their core business, what are things they should be automating? A good place to start would be automating data entry as it applies to sales deals, because it's a low cognition task. People either don't do it well, or they don't do it at all. Consequently, when looking at many CRM systems, the metrics are meaningless. The source information is incomplete because no one's entering the information properly.

So, if I look at an organization, that's the first thing: implement RPA around the CRM system, so sales staff can enter meaningful information about deals. This allows management to have accurate information towards the health of the company. The system being streamlined and automated frees up staff from spending hours in front of the CRM system. With hours free, staff can engage in trainings to boost and improve sales or focus on selling. Instead of looking at a screen trying to figure everything out, they can be solving problems for clients and customers.

While the changing work landscape can seem daunting to employees who are used to data entry or low cognitive work, the opportunity for growth and more fulfilling work causes greater job satisfaction in companies that are automating the repetitive tasks. Certain careers may disappear from the scene altogether once RPA takes off. Bookkeepers, data entry positions, auditing positions (where the employee is running a spreadsheet against payables/receivables), and other data processing jobs like that will be part of someone's five-minute cleanup task. For instance, if there is missing information, the Digital Worker will flag a specific necessary field for human interaction, instead of the whole task needing hands on.

Careers will require and inspire creativity. Candidates won't show up with certificates of completion for spreadsheet courses but will find their role within their applicable ways of applying knowledge to the field. Instead of being bored with the task oriented monotonous behaviors, employees will look at different ways to approach issues knowing that innovation and forward-thinking opportunities are rewarded and required.

Imagine the think tank environment that Google and other Silicon Valley tech firms are known for with quirky workplaces, sleep pads, funky tech and sensory rooms, just an all-around different work environment than is normative in most arenas...Now, imagine that freedom in industries everywhere. Tedious work being automated allows for more freedom. Obviously, a factory or restaurant may not be able to provide the same benefits as an office building might, but innovation in the mainstream may inspire it elsewhere. It only ever takes one successful risk taker to pave the way in an industry.

RPA—IT'S YOUR BUSINESS

RPA was designed to streamline business operations and reduce company costs. Automating simple processes frees up staff to complete higher value work and serve clients and customers better. Allowing RPA to handle little things, like autofill on forms and processing claims and complaints with fewer errors and frustration, to the big things, like audits and delivering reports after delving through copious amounts of data, maximizes efficiency and human capital while safeguarding the integrity of information with an organization.

Lacking customer presence by making decisions like outsourcing communication to other countries using autodial has become a norm. Business has already worked to cut corners and jokes abound about reaching customer service agents that don't speak the native language of the clients well. Allowing Digital Workers to handle the mundane tasks gives back to the budget for people to manage human touch points. Instead of waiting on hold to be misunderstood and feel frustrated, employees aren't managing large data sets, but are focused on helping clients so they can walk away feeling like they are with a company that cares.

Holistic over algorithmic approaches are forward thinking in outreach instead of reacting to problems. The Digital Worker automates algorithmic tasks. For instance, if a contract can't be signed until the signee is 21, the computer can check dates. The Digital Worker can also bring up fields that still need filled in on paperwork, point out where files may need uploaded and not push paperwork through to the next phase (or person) until the fields are completed. The Digital Worker is also able to send emails reminding someone to continue their application or paperwork to completion. If a few emails don't work to get the person back in front of the form, the Digital Worker can send an email to the correct employee to reach out to the person needing to complete the form, and the employee can take it from there. If an average employee would have to manage hundreds of these calls each day, the scope and reach of the employee would be limited. If the Digital Worker is doing the brunt of the work, the employee is free to reach out to the people who need human prompting or help. This example shows how one small task has many steps along the way and is just one small example of RPA capabilities.

The mother of all software is enterprise resource planning (ERP). ERP manages day-to-day business activities such as project management, procurement, accounting, risk management, compliance, and supply chain operations. A complete ERP suite will include enterprise performance management software that helps budget, plan, predict, and report on an organization's financial results. ERP can manage several locations for a company and centralizes data, usually in the cloud, so it can be accessed by anyone who needs it wherever they are geographically. These systems are capable of a lot of functions. RPA leverages ERP. Without ERP, RPA is still capable of handling these processes. RPA is capable within ERP with coding. Here, the Digital Worker acts as a maximizer for an all-encompassing software. Let's look at how the two systems can work in tandem.

ONBOARDING

For instance, Doug decides he's hiring Ella. Doug starts typing then logs into the HR system. Now, Ella will need a company email and a badge with accesses. RPA allows an optical reader to grab all scanned documents and fill in fields while Doug is still talking to Ella. The RPA can start generating the email and sending info to the badge printer. RPA can send the first email and make sure that the ERP system is updated with all pertinent information, so Mark, Ben, and Elizabeth can log in real-time and get updates on new hires. Doug can add notes to the HR file later, "Ella is incredibly knowledgeable and an asset to the sales team. We made a goal for her to sell (numerical goal) every quarter..." As Ella is exiting Doug's office, an HR manager can walk over and hand her paperwork, her badge, shake her hand and welcome her to the team warmly with a tour of the company.

This type of efficiency and professionalism saved everyone time, and Ella sees what to expect at Team Lanshore immediately. He also didn't miss out on positive human interaction. This approach saved her time moving from Doug's office to sitting in the HR office waiting for her turn to go through the hiring paperwork, waiting on a badge, and for someone to hand her an email and password. This can eat up half a day for some new hire processes. ERP and RPA being leveraged together created a lasting impression and good experience for Ella.

RPA is capable of doing this process alone, because it functions much the same. Even without

ERP software, a company can leverage RPA for similar or the same results.

ANALYTICS AND DATA

Without data, there is no reason for analytics. Analytics drives business. The Digital Worker becomes responsible for the process of detecting, deciphering, and communicating substantial patterns in data. In other words, analytics helps us discover connections and consequential links in data that might be overlooked without interpretation. The Digital Worker can monitor all factors within a company's branding and pull information from multiple social media outlets, compiling the data on marketing campaigns so money can be spent effectively and with better return on investment; the company wins. All the sudden, instead of having someone flipping from screen to screen trying to see which video, meme, post, or picture captured your target audience's attention, you're receiving the breakdown reports so you can maximize results with every post.

The Digital Worker is able to watch results in live time. If something goes viral, the Digital Worker could be set to notify management at one million views so the company can get ready for an influx and get started on engaging the audience. If something doesn't get any attention, the Digital Worker could alert someone in charge of social media management to delete the post and put up something more engaging.

Another way having a Digital Worker in charge of data and analytics is helpful is in decision making processes. For instance, the Digital Worker can scan the internet for information within set parameters. So, your company wants to add a product. What information exists? The Digital Worker can compile a report on the product family to give you an idea of costs associated with the product. The Digital Worker can find out if the product has ever faced lawsuits and why, what claims or reviews competitors have had, competition pricing and valuation, costs associated with making the product, and past available sales information. A person doing this level of research may need weeks to compile a report. The Digital Worker may need hours and can link you to all relevant information.

Maybe your company wants to restructure the way management looks, the Digital Worker can find information to manage the pros and cons for almost all situations, as long as someone from your team can define the search terms in a meaningful way for the data and analytics to be compiled for you. If you make tennis balls, you wouldn't want to define a search for 'balls,' that wouldn't give you a good vantage point of your industry.

DISPUTE RESOLUTION

One of the biggest problems in Commission Management (CM) is disputes in pay. This issue is valid and shows up when sales aren't captured correctly, or commission isn't calculated correctly. Investigating could take multiple screenshots, going through bills of sale. When call centers or human resources is involved, time is lost, and frustration levels rise as salespeople await a correction in their pay. Productivity can dip as a result, which can impact future sales. Dispute management with RPA consolidates data, sends a message saying the pay dispute is being processed, it's altogether less intrusive than involving different departments and having the salesperson run around getting frustrated by multiple people not having satisfactory answers.

A head of HR and Compensation shared with our team in Lanshore White Paper: *Profit Today from RPA in HR Operations*, "Compensation disputes are one of my biggest headaches. The time it takes to get together all the facts and compare system records makes an already contentious issue more aggravating for the employee who raised the dispute. And the costs of processing, questioning and arbitrating consume budget that needs to be invested in development, not firefighting. The sums involved make it a board-level issue."[1] Hearing from someone handling commission disputes puts the entirety of the problem into perspective. It's much more than missing money from a paycheck.

DISPUTE RESOLUTION CASE STUDY

The following is also found in the white paper. The impact of dispute management is the bottom line. A recent customer Lanshore worked with had 15,000 payees. In an average month, there would be 3,500 disputes submitted. The issue was arising as an average of fifteen days were needed to gather the information necessary to start an investigation into the dispute. As you can imagine, payees with disputes would get irritated that the process takes so long, which is understandable. No one wants their money messed with. The typical plan agreements allowed for the company to resolve a dispute within 90 days. The external dispute and system management was costing our client $3 Million per year. Internal staff costs were further exacerbating the problem to the tune of $5 Million each year. Dispute management error costs were accruing to $19 Million in annual financial leakage. That's a lot of money to be spending on mistakes. When our client had finally had enough of hemorrhaging $19 Million annually, they called Lanshore in to resolve the problem.

While the numbers are daunting, to say the least, let's consider the exasperation of disgruntled payees. The dispute resolution process being utilized required users to provide a considerable amount of information and evidence before submitting their dispute to the organization. The information being required was already held in systems around the business. Payees were reporting feeling undervalued by the company they care so much about because barriers requiring available information were barring their pursuit of fair compensation. The dispute process was unclear and undocumented past the submission of relevant proof and information provided by payees which caused more loss of time and unhappiness with the organization for the payees requiring dispute resolution.

To set the parameters for disputes that are suitable for bot processing, we carry out an initial automation evaluation. This identifies the potential processes, then assesses and scores them against RPA criteria, including repetitiveness, frequency, complexity, standardization, and documentation. This produces a cut-off score for requests that will be handled using automation and exceptions which will need manual intervention. We refine the processes, if necessary, to reduce the number of exceptions.

A centralized dispute inbox is monitored by an invoker robot. It parses parameters in the emails and sends them on to the bot server for automated processing. Automation requests are queued then processed by the next available robot. The results go back to the RPA server for monitoring and reporting.

The Head of HR and Compensation reported back on the differences that Digital Workers made: "Deploying RPA has made a big difference to our dispute resolution burden. We've cleared a backlog and got typical resolution times down from fifty to ten working days. Word's got around and the workforce is more confident in our ability to arbitrate fairly. That means less tension and more trust and productivity. Payees don't feel they have to keep chasing up – they know they'll get a reliable response. My team can focus on manually resolving only the exceptional or complex cases, so they can use their time on projects that support business growth."

Going from an average of fifty days until resolution to ten days is huge when considering paychecks were off. There were employees waiting on money they may have factored into budgets or needed to keep their households running. Leaving disputes unanswered for a prolonged amount of time can cause disruptions to the sales force and loss of incredible salespeople. Trust must exist between companies and the people working for them. The incentive to make sales is the paycheck, so when there's a problem with pay, especially if it's ongoing, the trust and motivation breakdown. The risk is not worth the loss of reward. If a Digital Worker, or seven, is the difference between continued success or a breakdown in forward movement, what are organizations waiting for?

On the next page you can see the comparison between the dispute resolution without and with RPA.

Spot the difference: timescales with RPA and without it

PAYEE SUBMITS
A DISPUTE
NO RPA ASSISTANT

Administrator logs into portal periodically to assign new disputes to analysts at random

Analysts log in to the portal periodically to review tickets assigned — **5 DAYS**

Analyst selects ticket to review and updates status to In Progress

Analyst pulls or requests data needed for review — **15 DAYS**

Analyst reviews and analyzes data set

Analyst approves or denies ticket and updates dispute status — **30 DAYS**

Analyst cannot resolve and escalates

Analyst sends email to submitter's manager

Analyst and manager resolve and update dispute status as Approved or Denied — **90 DAYS**

In this scenario, the process drags on for up to 90 days. It's entirely manually driven, so can be delayed by staff holidays and other tasks, mis-communication and human error within the resolution process.

The payee constantly has to check and chase to find out what's happening.

PAYEE SUBMITS
A DISPUTE
WITH RPA ASSISTANT

Bot assigns dispute to Analyst with least number of disputes

Bot sends notification emails — **1 MIN**

Bot pulls data from multiple sources

Bot compares data against defined criteria for approving, denying, or escalating

Bot approves or denies dispute ticket and updates status

Bot sends notification emails — **1-15 MIN**

Bot cannot resolve and sends notifications for human assistance

Analyst and manager resolve and update dispute status as Approved or Denied — **LESS THAN 15 DAYS**

In this scenario the data-gathering, basic decision-making and communication are all handled by the RPA bot. In a straightforward dispute, with all the data available from multiple sources, it can be resolved and notified within 15 minutes.

With a more complex or ambiguous situation, the data-gathering is still complete in minutes rather than weeks. Analysts and managers are freed from the upfront admin and can focus on resolving exceptional or complex cases, which speeds up their response time.

Even the most onerous cases can typically be resolved within two weeks, with clear information and progress updates provided to the payee throughout the process.

The drastic differences RPA made for our client are replicable for other companies and in other industries.

FRAUD DETECTION

Another area of incredible loss for companies is fraud. The Association of Fraud Examiners released 2018 numbers, relayed by Business Fraud Prevention. In the United States, organizations lose an average of five percent of their gross revenues to fraud annually. Occupational fraud frequency is found at 42% in private and small businesses as opposed to large corporations, non-profits, and government organizations. We will emphasize their findings, "The BIGGEST CONTRIBUTING FACTOR is LACK OF INTERNAL CONTROLS." Fraud becomes a crime of opportunity when proper checks and balances aren't in place. While it would be wonderful if employees were always honest and operating in the best interest of the organizations they worked for, it simply isn't the case.

There's more to consider from the same report. Corruption was the most common fraud occurring in 32% of businesses with less than 100 employees and 43% frequency in companies with more than 100 employees. Billing schemes were the second most common fraud. When owners and executives were the perpetrators, the fraud cost was extreme with a median loss of $850,000.[2]

The takeaway from the report was fraud detection is costly and usually a bigger problem when internal controls are not in place. Intimidation through threats and collusion make fraud easy to hide when key players in the organization can also be the perpetrators or the ones running the reports and answering to higher ups. Digital Workers can't be persuaded to turning a blind eye to data that sits outside parameters.

Lanshore was building a Digital Worker for a company awhile back, and in the testing phases, we decided to run the RPA on our own company finances. No one was expecting any results to pop up, because we have internal controls, but lo and behold the newly programmed Digital Worker caught a discrepancy. This time by matching internal calendars to business credit cards. The information pulled up was standard versus non-standard transactions. Anomalies get pulled out of the data and put into a digitized report for human eyes to be able to make determinations and audit. Non-standard transactions would be things like furniture stores, trips and airline tickets (which could very well be work related), and cash disbursements. Once the Digital Worker pulls out the non-standard transactions, the human audit begins. Instead of hundreds or thousands of entries to look at, increasing a margin of error, there are only non-standard transactions to rectify. The human can flag entries for more investigation or can be approved back into the ledger.

Fraud detection isn't something to be overlooked or ignored within organizations. The faster fraud is caught, the lower the costs associated through losses.

HANDLING MASSIVE SCALE FRAUD DETECTION

Enron shocked Wall Street and the world with massive fraudulent activity across the board: offshore accounts and businesses hiding funds and making deals, insider trading information allowing executives to dump stocks when they were at the top, accountancy issues with audits and hidden books, and so much more. Let's focus on two things: the measurable size of the fraud and how its relevant to RPA.

Publicly traded companies have a responsibility to their shareholders. The companies are run by individuals who may be focused on themselves, which is where Enron seems to have gone off the tracks. In 1996, Enron was reporting $13.3 billion in revenue which made a huge jump in 2000 $100.8 billion. In reality, the company was losing money, but with reported revenue increases in the billions, people were talking about Enron and investing in a company that seemed to be growing in leaps and bounds. 29 Enron executives and directors sold their shares, receiving $1.1 billion from the sale of a collective 17.3 million shares, all between 1999 through mid-2001.[3]

When the entire scandal came out everyone was pointing fingers at each other saying they didn't have the experience with accounting to know what was happening or they were fooled and didn't know anything was amiss. No one wanted to take responsibility for the bankruptcy and failure of billions of dollars.

According to a BBC Report, "One of the key checks on the way businesses operate is the external audit by accountants who inspect the books. In Enron's case, that was the firm of Arthur Andersen."[4] Anderson had won profitable bids from Enron and didn't want to risk ruining their business relationship by pointing out concerning findings on their client.

Corporate level fraud isn't isolated to the United States. Since 2001, the UK has witnessed high-profile accounting scandals where auditors have come under scrutiny: including BHS, Patisserie Valerie and Carillion in the UK.

Germany experienced a massive accounting scandal with electronic payments company Wirecard. They confessed €1.9bn (£1.6bn) of cash on the books "probably did not exist."[4] Again, the CEO pointed blame towards other avenues when confronted with fraud charges. So, how do shareholders ensure the companies they are invested in are financially stable? Is there a way to create a trustworthy measurable unbiased auditing system that removes issues seen in devastating fraud cases?

The answer is unequivocally, yes. It creates a new set of questions, but there could, hypothetically, be an auditing program made that looks into all financial facets of companies and balances the real time information with what is being portrayed to the public. This Digital Worker could be tied into a master system that streamlines data for each public company for shareholders and investors to see up-to-date financial reports. The Digital Worker would be set to find, analyze, and red flag transactions outside the norm of the organization. This would require an investigative team or for the company to upload information relative to transactions. A huge transfer to an offshore account would raise red flags. Changes in pay schedules for executives would be caught. Companies wouldn't be able to hide charitable contributions or exchanges with other companies, it would all become accessible and build accountability measures.

The big question becomes how do you measure the integrity and trustfulness of the company coding the RPA and storing the data? Could someone be bought off or could it be coded within the Digital Worker to catch even this level of corruption? It would be important to code a fail safe within the code that could catch a hacker to the Digital Worker and keep the integrity of the program. White collar crime is big money consequences. It would be interesting to see society change expectations for reporting systems. Instead of extreme losses devastating portfolios, RPA offers non-biased ways to bypass corruption. Unlike auditing companies and accounting firms, Digital Workers cannot be paid to look the other way or keep a second set of books. The Digital Worker increases all aspects of business when the vision exists for the programming.

LANSHORE RETAIL CASE STUDY—ENHANCING PRODUCTIVITY

2020 lockdowns created a surge in online ordering which created more demand for ways to help businesses be competitive in the retail space online.

Giants like Amazon, Walmart, etc. were already prepared and experienced in taking large amounts of orders, but smaller to mid-sized businesses needed to round a huge learning curve to be (or stay) competitive in their respective online retail spaces. Using RPA to eliminate backlogs and get orders to customers while managing inventory and reordering product in real time became necessary.

What were the challenges we dealt with in the past? Our client, in the retail apparel business, had to process a large number of customer orders downloaded from SharePoint to a spreadsheet. The data was not grouped by customer orders, so there was additional work when the spreadsheet was finally loaded. For each customer, an employee needed to go to the routing site and process the orders for the current customer (sometimes multiple orders per customer), then save the results of the released orders into a new tab of an Excel Spreadsheet. At the end of the process, they had to upload the spreadsheet, with the results of the released orders, then send a confirmation email. The full process was taking two resources around an hour apiece and was leading to backlogs.

How did Lanshore deliver retail RPA solutions? Lanshore was able to use RPA to replicate the process and reduce the time it takes down to eight minutes. Our client is looking into their processes for other ways to utilize RPA for efficiency.

The bottom line is anytime improvements can save time and money; they should be utilized. Small immediate gains add up over time. In any business, time is money. Money is either invested, earned, or wasted. Given a choice between profitability and growth versus a lack of self-awareness in the technological aspects of your business, there shouldn't be many choosing the latter option. Lanshore continues to give time back, that compounds. No investment pays the interest you could save by automating certain processes.

COMPLIANCE

When laws are passed dealing with compliance issues that have reporting requirements, RPA can help manage the deadlines and paperwork to ensure the company is compliant with both the issue and reporting. Accruing fines and legal fees for not being within the parameters can be costly.

European Union's General Data Protection Regulation (GDPR), California's air quality standard laws, or the United States' Health Insurance Portability and Accountability Act (HIIPA) require compliance and reports with deadlines. Failure to comply with these or hundreds of other regulatory demands can cause significant fines, reputational harm, and lost revenue. Non-compliance can cost more than paying to adhere to relevant regulatory rules.

Setting up Digital Workers as part of your Compliance Management Team can help keep track of data and compiling reports real-time and track deadlines for reporting, alerting key employees to do anything on their end that may need the human touch.

Industry and company standards and audits for compliance by department or facility can also be met through the help of RPA. Allowing the Digital Worker to oversee data sets ensures that reports aren't influenced by humans trying to keep their jobs or earn performance bonuses. Ultimately, tampering with data in audits and reports does happen, for a plethora of reasons. RPA can cut down on discrepancies and give a better audited view of company standings and compliance with requirements.

DIGITAL WORKERS IN MANUFACTURING: LANSHORE CASE STUDY

The challenges our client faced the difficult challenge of having several business-critical processes finished daily. The only option available, before RPA, was to have employees completing these processes during working hours, which took them away from other vital duties that were being neglected for running processes. There was a marked adverse effect on production was costing the business valuable revenue.

Through implementation of RPA, Lanshore was able to automate seven key processes, across three manufacturing sites. The RPA ran these reports during non-working hours, yet still supplied the data in a compiled and organized way for use for the manufacturer.

All values will reflect the annual time savings for the three manufacturing locations affected positively by RPA Processes:

MRP Process:
Original Process Time (OPR): 1 person-70 minutes each day, Monday to Friday.
RPA Run Time: 50-55 mins for 3 sites (not during working hours)
DIFFERENCE: OPR 910 hours/year during working hours while RPA delivered in 650-715 hours/year during non-working hours, leaving the 910 labor hours available for the key employees to be on the manufacturing floor.

Liberation PLS Process:
Original Process Time: 1 person, 4h-5h every Thursday (with a loss of 4-5 hours work) per location.
RPA Run Time: 3h- 3h30m (not during working hours)

Impression Work orders process:
Original Process Time: 1 person, 2-3 hours every Friday to print work orders and plans per location.
RPA Run Time: 1-1.5 hours

Projections Process:
Original process time: 1 person, 1-2 hours every Friday creating the report needed, per location.
RPA run time: 10-20 minutes

Smooth Sand Process:
Original process time: 1 person, 1-2 hours every Thursday creating the report needed.
RPA run time: 10-20 seconds

Requisitions Process:
Original process time: 1 person, more than 1 hour per day
RPA run time: 20-40 minutes

ROP Process:
Original process time: 1 person, 1 hour, or more, per purchase order
RPA run time: around 20-30 minutes

THE FUTURE OF MANUFACTURING RPA

Our client was pleased with the outcomes of the RPA that was applied to the business processes. They have decided to have Lanshore develop RPA for several more processes. The automation of reports has allowed their employees to focus on their billable work, greatly increasing departmental efficiency, which has the byproduct of benefiting other departments. Running processes outside of work hours, (01:00. 02:00, and 05:00) prepares the data and documents needed for each day of work, before employees even arrive at the office. There has been an obvious leap in job satisfaction due to less interruptions and more ability for the company to give back to their employees as their profit margins rise.

Manufacturing runs best when the machines never stop. When someone is out of their place, even to run necessary reports, the line slows down or halts, which equals loss of revenue. Manufacturing companies must outpace their global competitors to not only offer better products at competitive prices, but also to have a competitive edge in the workforce to attract great employees capable of driving organizational goals. Without vision and a plan to make these things possible, a manufacturing plant could easily become an empty building. RPA is the solution.

LANSHORE CASE STUDY: SOFTWARE COMPANY: TERRITORY TRACKING AND INCREASING SALES

In any company, there are many challenges that take creative solutions to streamline multiple moving parts and create continuity and integrity of data. Without having multiple people manipulating data and focusing on keeping errors within files low, productivity and ability to advance corporate goals becomes difficult.

The first problem that Lanshore identified and tackled with our client was the lack of an automated feed to upload territories through an ODI process to maintain a strawman to track the territory definitions. The tedious process in place to update around 300 territories individually took around seven to fifteen minutes per territory. These territories changed daily over a tracked period of five months.

HOW DID LANSHORE DELIVER RPA FOR STREAMLINING THIS COMPLICATED PROCESS?

Automating the 300 plus territories for daily runs made the eight-to-twelve-hour daily process, by two employees, a twenty-minute process each day.

RPA automated the extraction of the Excel files, defined by the developer, and automatically updated the information in the system. Our client was given a cost-effective way to execute reports and files while freeing up great employees to focus on more important projects. The RPA also forecasts the plan payouts that were more difficult to project due to the changing territories.

The time savings looks like this in this case: 2,080-3,120 hours per year on these daily reports was reduced to 86.67 hours per year on the same reports. The efficiency of the RPA process was also able to account for changing territories and less confusion that often-accompanied manual entry of data.

ADDITIONAL CHALLENGES MET BY LANSHORE'S RPA SOLUTIONS

Our client had annual Final Territory Reports that had to be run for various reasons at end of year: Tax purposes, profit loss, building a game plan for the next year, sending financial documents to various entities and individuals, etc. The level of these final reports was in-depth and included many data driven checks and balances that took painstaking time to complete. The original process time was three full weeks of work, eight plus hours per day, by two people. The employees dreaded this time of year and finalizing these reports because it was very tedious monotonous number crunching. Lanshore created an RPA process that was able to successfully finish the 240 hours' worth of work in a mere 4 hours. The employees expressed gratitude that they didn't have to spend weeks doing these final reports anymore.

This next bit is technical but included to show the scope of RPA. Our client didn't have the ability to download the definition of territories from the UI, as SAP didn't have that feature. Not all of their Compensation Admins have access to UI or know how to use the Callidus system. This made territory exporting almost impossible to achieve, but necessary for daily work to be accomplished. Through implementation of RPA, Lanshore has automated the login process to UI and gave RPA the ability to copy/paste the territories into an Excel spreadsheet. The bot only takes five minutes to do this, allowing Compensation Admins to use this file for their investigations and modifications without delays in the process.

Our client has an extensive look-up table with 50 indexes. The table expands annually with additional indexes. Our client's employees had to version each cell, add new values, replacing any old cells, which is a time-consuming process. Human error in these processes skews any results. This process would take three days to complete, when it was necessary, and included human error. Lanshore's RPA solution efficiently added all necessary cells and info, updated the values, without any error, in just two hours (instead of the 24 hours manually, with mistakes). Compensation Admins were able to utilize the reports and compare against original values much more quickly and come to closure on validations.

When RPA is utilized to execute processes that tie up key employees from completing tasks that drive other processes' success or failure, time is of the essence. Efficiency and the ability to have vital information at the fingertips of decision makers, at all times, with accuracy, changes the way companies build and compete in the global market. The challenge with RPA is applying it correctly to automating your vital processes. Once you get that done, the focus is on growth and retention.

Chapter 5

Education Automation

As a society that values education at every level of life, from early childhood through university to continuing education for licenses and entire industries, there is a clearly a need for RPA inside the education sector. Digital Workers aren't new to education. The first Digital Worker was the Scantron. "Only use a #2 pencil, fill in the entire bubble, and only one per line, so your test scores will reflect your grade correctly." The younger generations may never understand now that online tests exist, but we acknowledge the dinosaur in education that made grading multiple-choice exams much faster and easier on teachers and professors everywhere.

The proposal for educational purposes and RPA isn't as much for grading as for dealing with management of students. RPA isn't going to assist teachers in grading subjective matters. It isn't going to read a math proof and catch that the work is brilliant, but one calculation was missed, assessing partial credit and a note about the great work but a sloppy error. RPA won't read essays and respond with passion and emotion to the grand points made within the paper.

What a Digital Worker would do very well in the educational system is help manage the disciplinary system and help steer students into the correct programs/courses for their needs. There could be an amazing way to incorporate RPA into the recruitment and athletics departments of schools. Let's break down the possibilities and then look at a case study of how we helped at the university level already.

DISCIPLINE

Labels in schools help some students while making life difficult on other students. A student labeled a "troublemaker" may find themselves on the wrong side of the principles desk often, which may lead to harsh punishments for small infractions. This could lead to more acting out and more trouble for the "troublemaker," while a student known for good behavior and great grades might get away with a horrible decision that should have had consequences.

Consistency in the area of discipline could raise morale and respect from students and parents alike. Different people can handle the same problem in different ways. For instance, a student walks into Mr. Z's classroom chewing gum. Mr. Z takes a trash can over and silently waits for the student to spit the gum into the bin. The same student walks into Mrs. Y's classroom chewing gum and she just ignores the student blowing bubbles in class. Same student with gum in Miss X's class gets asked by Miss X for a piece. Then in study hall, gets sent to the office for having gum for the third day. The student didn't change. The circumstance didn't change; the student was chewing gum in every instance. The teacher changed and with the teacher, the approach to the gum chewing changed. This could be very confusing for a student.

All schools have handbooks serving as the guideline for what is expected and the consequences for not meeting a standard. If so many days are missed by a good student and a "bad student," it would not be fair for the good student to get a gentle reminder to not miss anymore days while the "bad student" sits in detention for a week. RPA could be leveraged to deliver a report that holds no bias to any student, just a list: "These students have missed X number of days, and according to school code ABC, they must report for 3 days of detention." The Digital Worker could also print out the forms that go home for each student and log their detentions served to track the next level of disciplinary action that would need taken if the behavior continued. Then, there is no determination based on discrimination, just fair measures matching the circumstances. The valedictorian could be sitting next to the stoner in detention, and neither could claim they were singled out.

Obviously, there are tons of issues that schools have to deal with, and this isn't meant to be comprehensive overview of school correction policies. The point is discipline shouldn't be biased, and teachers, principals, administrators, and parents have bad days. At the beginning of the day, the principal may feel more forgiving than before the last bell when they are ready to go home. This isn't a character problem, just part of being human. What happens in a school system where the character of the person or people in charge of discipline does have bad character? What if they favor males over females or vice versa? What if they let everything the athletes do wrong slide so they can compete, thus causing others to be resentful, creating a hostile school environment? What if they have favorite students getting away with bullying? What if…?

There are different scenarios playing out all over the place, which is why discipline in schools could benefit from RPA comparing the handbook to measures taken in the past with students. Then Butch isn't getting suspended for days over something that Jimmy got a warning for. The RPA system would take the information input and make a determination after levying all information appropriately and without emotion. "The options in this case are a detention, a letter home, and/or a session with the school counselor to make a plan for positive decision making in conflict resolution with peers." Obviously, as behavior escalates, the Digital Worker would escalate with the school policy requirements and according to past disciplinary measures.

Creating fairness in discipline and opportunity within education takes stress off the decisionmakers, students, and their parents. RPA could ensure the accusation of partiality, prejudice, discrimination, excessive and inequitable punishment was removed from the system. The Digital Worker could easily be audited for all similar decisions making any lawsuits or public concerns could be dealt with. The only issues would be immediate updating to the system so that the RPA could do its job correctly. The various reports that RPA could manage would also paint a clear picture for where resources may need allocated within the school district, for instance a high rate of fights in the parking lot may require cameras be added in places to catch the behaviors. A security guard may be needed in certain locations but may be unnecessary in others.

PLACEMENT

There are incredibly ambitious students that loudly state what they want and there are brilliant quiet students who might be ready for new opportunities, but they may not vocalize their interest in the opportunities. RPA could assess school records, at all levels, and catch students that qualify for various programs offered, printing off the information to be given to them. These assessments might only be necessary before scheduling classes or once a year, depending on when the opportunities begin. Instead of relying on teacher recommendations or student interest, RPA can quickly run analytics to find who qualifies for what—accelerated and otherwise. This also eliminates discrimination of opportunity or favoritism.

Many schools utilize a form of RPA for class scheduling, although some look at each student individually and have to figure out what they still need and when it's offered to complete requirements for graduation or advancement. If a school doesn't have some level of RPA for scheduling, they need it immediately.

Accurate assessments of a student's potential can propel students to new heights and help the schools focus on the needs of all the students. Test scores for schools are important for funding needs, and RPA could help figure out what students need more or less in areas of concern. There are many benefits to having precise reports run more often without taxing already overworked staff and teachers. An RPA system connecting the different factors affecting education (attendance, grades, disciplinary record, numerical data tracing concerns and points of interest in a student's life, etc.) could help with the overall wellbeing of the schools, staff, students, and their families throughout the educational process and lifetime.

ATHLETICS

Imagine any sports movie. The coaches come to the locker room to motivate the athletes for a win. Charts with Xs and Os mark plays, and the coach animates the paths with flare and excitement as he shows possible cuts across the field and what to expect from competitors. Some movies show them analyzing the opposing team's videos and building huge playbooks and stats on all opponents. This gets painstaking when you consider how many games each team plays and that there is a change in players every year while coaches maintain their style, that certain teams may run certain plays in specific situations, and it is information overload to remember every detail.

RPA could store information and run statistics real time. Professional teams may already utilize a program for this, but it would take high school and collegiate sports to a whole new level if there was an

RPA system available for all teams. The playing field would change drastically as every decision was optimized for outcome on both sides. Imagine knowing the likelihood of potential plays in a situation based on score, who is on the field/floor. The program could even track the tendencies of individual players, much like score keeping on paper, where someone tracks every play and outcome to be analyzed later. One person could be keeping book live while the information was streaming t the coaches RPA and spitting out real time possibilities to the coach. Past and present games would be built into spreadsheets and videos making the team and coaches more adept during the games.

Recruiting for athletics, for schools that are allowed and at the collegiate level, could take on a whole new and competitive look with RPA. A school that put emphasis on academics and athletics could screen grades better. Schools that need certain positions filled on their roster would get a printout of possibilities. If all the schools were using a centralized place for stats, it could make collegiate recruiting incredible for smaller schools that don't normally see recruitment efforts from colleges, thus enhancing smaller school opportunities for their athletes. Levelling the playing field is about more than more wins for the big guys on campus, it could revolutionize the sports arena, as we know it. Since athletes get opportunities for scholarships, it could help small town athletes get more exposure for their futures, helping some that wouldn't go to college get the opportunity while others might've gone to college and a scholarship would lower their financial responsibility and the loans they would have taken out.

UNIVERSITIES AND RPA

Discipline, placement, scheduling, and athletics at the university level all benefit from RPA much like we've already explained. The only differences would be in the scheduling department: They already operate with RPA on some level to keep all the students' different degree paths, with majors and minors, in line with what they need to graduate. This enables the academic advisors to run the program and explain when things are offered annually to assist in the best scheduling choices. The RPA gives the advisor more time to ask how the student is, and the personal touch may make the difference for some students when it comes to recognizing where help (mental health or academically) may be necessary. "How are you?" goes a long way in showing concern and is more productive than chasing down information that can and should be digitized and giving logical options for best case scenarios in the scheduling department.

Smaller universities can utilize RPA for adding quality students to their rosters. In a world of Big Ten schools, lists of party schools, universities with prestige, and countless other enticing extras, a smaller college cannot afford to lose the opportunity to be in touch with potential students, which leads us to a case study where we worked with a university to maximize their contact with the people looking into their offering.

RPA allows universities to handle more students—in person and online. The most important stat is the graduation rate. RPA helps in determining the trajectory of students in classes and helps plan a more direct path to graduation with a degree instead of thirty art classes and a knucklehead that needed Biology I, II, Chemistry I, II, Microbiology I, II, and several other science classes all stacked in two years but not in the right semesters. The future Microbiologist with a minor in Botany is probably going to need to evaluate the original goals and either take longer to graduate or change trajectory.

Most colleges and universities have a program that runs goals against what's available. It could be improved upon by creating faster graduating schedules together for the highly motivated that also allowed them to play with electives to fit a minor or two into their interests. Any way to add to the offering while maximizing the ultimate goal (graduation) is a win-win for the student and the school. Success in mind planning of RPA challenges the utilization of better RPA with more productive functionality and additional options for the users and to maximize the end result (more classes taken which is more revenue while ensuring graduation). There are many other ways to maximize RPA within the educational landscape. The model just mentioned could be replicable for intern placement and careers available for alumni with local businesses or far outside the local reach, maybe this type of innovative application of RPA drives global career opportunities for alumni of colleges that have created leadership by their practices and what they pass on to their graduates.

LANSHORE CASE STUDY: UNIVERSITY RPA SYSTEM

A smaller university reached out to us to help figure out why their enrollments were down and to find why there was minimal engagement through their website from possible students. The problem wasn't their website, but the management of the information captured on their website. We found that an average of twenty people per day were filling out the forms to request more information about the university, starting the application process without finishing, or were asking to be contacted because they had questions regarding filling out the application.

When we sat down with the key decision makers, we asked, "Who handles the information coming in from the site?"

After looking around at each other, someone finally offered, "Jill from HR used to handle that, but now I don't know who is managing it."

Therein was the problem. No one was calling potential students and the information about the data captured on the site was being stored on the site, not sent to someone for further review. The only time the information was managed was when someone went searching for the data and then did something with it, which turned out to be something no one was handling.

Before RPA, their process was an employee would have to go into the website and run a report.

Only one person knew where to access the report, and her workload didn't always afford her the time to print out the information. When she was available for this extra task, she would have to read and interpret all of the information and make calls as her time allowed. Unfortunately, due to the demands of her job, she wasn't keeping up with the reports and calls, and the university was dropping thousands of potential students because of lack of follow-up. That was unacceptable, but a problem created by lack of human capital. The loss of possible tuition meant trimming the fat instead of hiring another person to manage communication on the website, which turned into a cyclical issue.

Boiled down, the challenge was our client had an issue losing track of prospective students that were not completing the online forms, but were leaving them for a later time, then not returning to the form due to forgetfulness or closing out browsers. Dropped contact with prospective students could cause them to look elsewhere, especially if they aren't reengaged in the enrollment process. The process for contacting students that had begun the process was non-existent, because the people that were expected to do this were incredibly busy helping students in-person at the campus. With the challenge clearly identified, we began the road to the solution.

Our client's process, when we started, was a downloadable Excel Report that contained a list of students that applied for the college but had not finished the application. Each student had to be validated in the Students Management System. That was where this process became tedious for busy employees on campus. If the email of the student was registered in the system, the bot we created would continue processing the next student. If the email was not already in the system, the bot would then register the student into the system. At the end of the process, a confirmation email gets sent to a list of specified email addresses. This process would normally take a university employee an hour to complete, more if there was a larger number of students that didn't complete the application. RPA reduced the run time to three minutes.

Throughout the data capture process, emails could be sent. So, if someone was looking for information, a data capture of their email would be the first step, and an email based on what they had indicated would be sent. The system was set to a timed follow-up in stages, that had interactive prompts to propel a prospective student to more engagement with the website application. The auto-response emails structurally changed what the university was doing to help the prospective student finish what they had started.

THE CHANGING EDUCATIONAL LANDSCAPE

Universities have a unique opportunity to utilize RPA to enhance their antiquated systems. Covid-19 has changed the educational landscape. It seems that only the most technologically advanced institutions may survive an online world.

After complete shutdowns in 2020, the digital landscape of education should be of utmost importance to all educational institutions. Can they convert to entirely online processes to propel students towards graduation and keep them enrolled? While a full return to normalcy is ideal, it should remain forefront in our minds that being ready for challenges that come along, outside of the normal realm of control, must be planned for in the name of longevity. RPA is a great starting point for making headway towards automation that makes sense. Handing over the reins to repetitive, time consuming, rule-based tasks ensures they get done and in less time so human capital can be focused where its needed. Allowing important processes to slip through the cracks because someone doesn't have time can be the difference between thriving and going belly up.

THE FUTURE OF JOBS AND THE IMPLICATIONS FOR EDUCATION

Automation is taking away more and more work based on repetitive processes. Being hirable at an organization will require cognitive thought, whereas in the past, jobs were more accessible to people with lower IQ. Certain jobs are set to disappear from the offering, like data processing. Knowing how to approach problems and solve them effectively is imperative when task-oriented jobs are being taken over by Digital Workers.

Watching Jordan Peterson talk about the jobs different IQs can excel in reiterated what we already knew coming into the writing of this book. No one wants to address that there are people that are unemployable. It is easier to tell others to pull themselves up by the bootstraps or plan on training people to do what they aren't capable of, which is cruel. It is more merciful to admit there are unemployable humans that need a different solution, like an experimental minimum income that ensures they don't go hungry or end up homeless when they aren't capable of working in a digitally transforming era. Of course, there will still be a need for worker bees, so to speak, but higher cognition employees will be sought after.

Peterson's premise was there are hierarchies of competence, much like a pyramid. People with IQs between 116-130 (and above) are at the top of the pyramid. They are the one in eight to thirty and can manage careers that require more creativity, intelligence, conscientiousness, etc. As he worked through the different IQ levels, the jobs available to people got more repetitive and he admitted that automation would take their jobs eventually.[1] Where does that leave them?

Peterson references IQ for the military, and the point is valid, although due to branch specific differentiations, we will address soldiers must score in certain percentiles to be inducted into their chosen branch. There are varying levels of work in the military and during wartime, numbers matter. So, if someone scores in a way making them incapable of serving a lower-level job in the military, what is left in the civilian world?

The military conducted an experiment called Project 100,000, also dubbed McNamara's Boys, in 1966, during the height of the Vietnam War. They lowered the standards to get more recruits prepared to fight on the frontlines. 354,000 were brought into the military under this new guideline restructuring. Of those men and women, half of those that went to Vietnam were delegated to combat units. Almost 6,000 of them died, which was a fatality rate three times that of regular recruits.[2]

The endeavor was originally pitched as part of the Johnson Administration's "War on Poverty." Here was a way to employ people who had otherwise been kept from the opportunity of gaining discipline through the Armed Forces. The idea was the discipline established in the military would train the newly included recruits and set them on a trajectory towards success in the future. Eyewitness accounts tell an entirely different story: Novelist Larry Heinemann, who served with the 25th Infantry Division in Vietnam, remembered in a 2005 memoir that at basic training barracks at Fort Polk, Louisiana, he would watch McNamara's Boys from across the street, "These were the guys who could not hack it during regular basic training. It was painful to watch....Some of them could not even get the hang of so simple a thing as standing at attention, and otherwise seemed severely unsuited for military life."[2]

Joseph Galloway, war correspondent awarded a Bronze Star with Valor for carrying wounded men to safety in the Battle of the Ia Drang Valley said the men from Project 100,000 couldn't read, had to be taught to tie their boots, failed training over and over until someone gave the greenlight to send them overseas. He recounts, "They could not be taught any more demanding job than trigger-pulling, [so most of them] went straight into combat, where the learning curve is steep and deadly."[2] These are the people we must prepare for in the workforce. The question is how? If they have to be taught how to tie their shoes and they can't read as adults, what is there for them? It is a bleak question that gets sidestepped, because it is much easier to cast blame at teachers and parents than admit there are people that aren't capable of normal tasks. That isn't the question of this book, but it moves us into the point of preparing the people who are able to function in the workforce to be employable into the future where automation is taking over.

Citizen developers will be necessary. When basic coding and computer skills become part of basic curriculum (which is already happening across the world), future employers are already engaging with technology in a way that prepares them to leverage higher brain function tasks in the future, which increases work output and efficiency for the employer.

Data entry jobs, bookkeeping, accounting, any repetitive work will be going away in the future. What can people do to maintain job security? Learn to code RPA. Go-getters understand they have to be on the cutting edge when job elimination happens. The clear value of automation is to put information at the fingertips of the people that need it. There is a general sense that automation is bad because of job elimination. The assumption is it's a job killer, and all these people will find themselves out of work as automation is scaled at organizations of every level in different institutions. The truth is the job industry will see a boost, as it always has when automation hits the scene. Things have always gotten better not worse. For instance, when the car industry eliminated livery workers, there were thousands of jobs created for every horseshoe maker and horse trainer.

When repetitive tasks are automated, we can put people to work in specialized ways. The consumption of goods is staggeringly diverse. Keeping good minds wrapped up in copy/paste, run reports, repeat mode, seriously undermines hidden talent and potential.

Let's look at just the whole food market. It isn't just a vast variety of raw fruits, vegetables, and grains, but hundreds of types of chips, puffs, crackers, breads, pastries. This takes innovation within a brand to say, "Hey, bleu cheese crumble fried pickle with dusted vinegar kettle chips is going to be a hit." Initially, that sounds overwhelming, but playing with the recipe and taste testing may show that this is a winner. More people are needed to create the new products and opportunities within organizations. Digital Workers aren't going to turn on one day and say they accidentally mixed two foods and the flavor combination might sell well. They can make sure the copy/paste and reporting on repeat are done so human capital is moved into innovation. Then, when it's time to make said kettle chips, people will be employed in manufacturing, product management from beginning potato and ingredients to sealed bag, sales, shipping, etc. Jobs weren't lost, people were reallocated to higher cognition tasks.

Companies that subscribe to RPA and digital transformation footprint changes will look at candidates and say, "If this is where we stand on these issues, we need to accentuate the hiring process by only hiring candidates that understand their value isn't in the tasks that can be automated, but in their thought processes and execution of their jobs, plus how they integrate the available applications into their work."

There are classes available for programming tools, fixing machinery, but they don't have Thought Provoking Conversations 101 available. An employee who has vision for their role within an organization and is always applying their talents and capabilities to the organization's goals is going to be what companies are looking for. Project 100,000 shows that despite the belief that you can train anything into most anyone, the reality is that some have it, some don't and the ones that do will be contributing to the care of the ones that don't. The only thing left is acknowledging that and doing better within the education system by offering more cognitive thought and coding courses so the ones that are capable can excel. Having a data entry class or a bookkeeping class, at this point in the tech world, would be pointless. Education needs to make sure they are changing with the times and offering courses that keep their students competitive in the workforce as the future continues to evolve technologically.

Chapter 6

Fear the Future or Learn the Future:

Digital Workers in the Government

Government entities don't have the same goals as businesses. Government doesn't have to please shareholders or make a profit. The role of government entities is to protect and serve the constituents at the respective level of service: local, state, or federal. Due to many government officials being elected, constituency satisfaction with job performance affects future votes. The government sector will deal with budget cuts and allocating funding and grants to the proper areas. RPA helps with budget control and allows additional productivity with existing staff. Improving efficiency of services and communication with the citizens is vital for the satisfaction of the area. Costs associated with implementing RPA is value based on goodwill. Improving citizenry engagement by allowing for less wait times for things like licenses and dealing with government employees can improve the happiness felt by constituents. RPA provides time for staff to help citizens because they aren't bogged down running multiple screens.

The ability for RPA to change lives in the government sector is seemingly limitless. We will cover different areas of interest, a case study of the RPA we designed, and projects we see transforming public servant roles and the safety and security of citizens with innovative RPA. Agencies within government have money pouring in that must be accounted for. Agencies are often working on grants to get more money for their projects or lobbying to get their projects on the list for more money. Digital Workers can help keep things rolling while the people make it to the meetings that get the projects important to the agency in front of the people needed to advance said projects for constituents.

The massive size of the federal level of government makes centralizing and connecting certain processes incredibly difficult. While there is great need for RPA at all levels and the benefits would far outweigh the challenges, it should be noted that local and state levels are far easier to get started with new technologies. So, we will focus our attention to the local and state level processes, which are also highly accountable to local constituents.

COURT SYSTEMS

Within the court system, there are many areas that can be addressed with RPA. The two most prevalent issues are collections of fees and judgments and the release of prisoners on the criminal side in a timely fashion. Many of the systems between groups don't communicate, and it causes delays and misunderstandings resulting in legal actions or issues with licensures or other things affected by paperwork errors. The biggest problem is that there is no small error when people's lives and livelihood are affected.

Within the court system, many of those found guilty must pay a judgment. The job of collecting that money falls to a court clerk. Typically, relevant information about a judgment is held in multiple systems. This means that the clerk must access those systems and validate the information before being able to accept a payment or arrange a payment plan. If the process of accessing the various systems takes too long, this creates a risk that the person waiting will become impatient and leave the court, thus delaying the collection of the judgment.

Using RPA, a bot would compile all necessary documents and check all systems for relevant information, pulling it all to one place for the clerk to access. This could happen as soon as a judgment is passed. The clerk would then be able to accept payment or arrange a payment plan without double checking multiple systems. The payment would also process and update all relevant files so there was no further issues for the person that had just taken care of their fines or fees.

Accounting of unpaid fees and fines would be made easier as well. Options to pay online already exist, but RPA would ensure updates were made to all systems, which can't happen when systems don't communicate. Many systems without RPA create a spreadsheet of online payments that need updated in multiple systems. Human error could cause a disruption to the files of people paying online, which causes headaches and frustration that is unnecessary with RPA streamlining simple processes.

Another huge issue is release papers not being sent or received in a timely fashion. The jail systems aren't synced with the court systems causing delays in releases which causes legal ramifications for the court system. Automating updates to speak to the jail information system after judges sign off on releases or order holds on inmates, safeguards inmates getting out by delayed hold orders being relayed or inmates being kept longer than they should. Errors are usually in the transmission of reports when these mistakes happen. Either the email/fax doesn't go through in time for the right thing to be done or is only transmitted during a certain timeframe while things can change hourly.

Auditing transitions and tracking changes is vital to being able to manage possible lawsuits in the future and can eliminate human error as long as updates are made in the system immediately. Streamlined systems can allow a judge to click a button and hit send updating all connected files. The expediency necessary when dealing with pressing issues like the justice system can revolutionize the entire process.

ASSISTANCE AND BENEFITS PROGRAMS

Most assistance programs are administered at the state or local level. As of 2011, there were 79 different means-tested welfare programs in the US. Many of the requests for welfare are submitted via paper forms, which humans must process. Also, because there are so many different areas of welfare, there's a need to transfer data from one system to another. To accomplish that, there are two choices: either make the welfare recipient fill out a form for each different benefit or have a person in the department whose transfers, via copy/paste, information from one system to another. This type of re-keying presents an opportunity for considerable streamlining with the use of RPA.

RPA could also look at the rule-based information (income, people in the home, and any other relevant variables like age, employment status, etc.) and show the employee what the person applying for benefits qualifies for across the assistance board. This would help the government worker click boxes based on the needs of the family to help them gain the assistance that fits their criteria.

In 2015, the United States Census Bureau reported that 52.2 million people received government assistance per month in 2012.[1] According to the United States Budget Committee reports this swallows up more than ONE TRILLION dollars per year.[2] That's across over 80 available programs, which means a lot of accounting and auditing is necessary. RPA could save a lot of time and headache for local, state, and federal employees.

FORESEEABLE HEADACHES

The biggest challenge to adopting RPA is that information must be clean and precise to ensure that the Digital worker is statistically correct and accurate with any computations and reports. Foundational to the success of implementing RPA is the ability of entry mistakes to be fixed in a timely manner. The Digital Worker isn't able to fix errant entries, but parameters can be set to catch anomalies in data sets. The challenge would pass to a human to find the correct data and make changes to the information.

LANSHORE CASE STUDY ON A LOCAL GOVERNMENT SCALE

The challenge call answered was in the Probate sector, our client, a County Government Agency, had to run two large reports daily, converting them from PDF Format into a single report that was required to be updated daily to show the information across county. The entire process would take three employees two days to complete, for a total of 18 hours. For the duration of the information checking and transfer of new information, the three employees were unable to work on other projects, and the work was tedious, time consuming, and boring.

HOW DID LANSHORE DELIVER RPA FOR PROBATE PROCESSES?

By automating the reports, the run time was reduced to two minutes for this process.

Over the course of the year, 936 work hours on these daily reports were reduced to the RPA finishing the work in 1 hour 45 minutes total. This left hundreds of hours for employees to focus on more satisfying work and projects.

As a direct result of the increased departmental efficiency in probate, our client automated more processes. Cost efficiency and time savings have proven that RPA is superior to manually entering the reports. Resources (time and money) are being utilized elsewhere in the department while key employees affected by the changes have reported increased job satisfaction and less time away from the office, which is an unmeasurable savings.

ADDITIONAL CHALLENGES MET BY RPA SOLUTIONS

Our client decided to advance RPA into their civil and criminal reporting systems, after achieving success with the probate side. The scope of the work was downloading reports from Odyssey, comparing the values against stored reports, extraction of amounts from scanned checks, that amounted to a lot of open screens and data entry points that required scrolling and double checking to ensure that the correct cells were filled in, to complete files and run comprehensive reports. Once this was completed, information was stored in consolidated Excel spreadsheet files that were sent out to key employees that then could manipulate data, but all receivers wouldn't have the changes unless and until each person emailed updated files that didn't consolidate all changes. At the end of each month, a few employees would compare values and ensure a variance of zero.

This process was eating up two hours every day, five days each week.

LANSHORE DELIVERS RPA TO ENHANCE CIVIL AND CRIMINAL REPORT PROCESSES

Lanshore automated the reports, reducing the run time for this process to 15 minutes each week. Over the course of a year, 520 work hours were reduced through RPA to 13 hours total. This freed up hundreds of additional hours of time to be spent on more fulfilling projects and increased job satisfaction.

When resources and expertise are freed up, to the tune of 1,441.25 hours, time can be better spent increasing constituent face time with key employees that were stuck behind desks for menial work before RPA was instituted. Furthermore, new initiatives and projects increasing constituent happiness and employee job satisfaction were able to be given the attentiveness and time that are required to improve other areas within the government sector.

When politicians keep their promises to better the communities they are elected to serve, and those changes are measurable, reelection becomes easier. RPA gives a collective advantage across the board.

SILVER TSUNAMI

Workforce issues facing government organizations (and the private sector) are recruiting qualified staff and retaining them, successful succession planning, and the development of personnel. These reoccurring concerns are intensified by the 'Silver Tsunami.' Baby Boomers have reached retirement with approximately 10,000 people nationwide turning 65 every day. "In fact, by the year

2020, for the first time in U.S. history, the number of Baby Boomers will surpass the number of children five years of age or younger, and by the year 2030, the population of adults over the age of 65 is expected to double."[3] With this inevitable stream of priceless tenured personnel retiring, government agencies must be proactive in putting a plan in place to hire and onboard future personnel before knowledge transfer prospects have vanished. Without the passing of the torch, so to speak, of valuable experience and training, optimizing the future generations of employees in government will be much more difficult than if planning curbs the imminent loss of the key players in organizations by ensuring their successors know how to follow in the tenured personnel's footsteps. There is no substitute for experience gained on the job, but training and sharing of knowledge is vital for success.

The government is still one of the careers that offers a pension to retirees when they have put in their time, and some government employees opt to retire earlier than 65, due to having two decades in. The human shortage as many people holding positions retire en masse means not enough replacements are coming. There have been retirement planning and delayed retirement incentives put in place to attempt to slow down the mass exodus of retirees from their positions without their replacement in position. Government pensions are the reason some people choose government jobs making less annually over making more annually with no pension in the private sector. In small localities, federal offices choose to close rather than train a whole new staff when their leaders and everyone under them are retiring relatively close together. Other regions swallow up the smaller regions which causes more work for already swamped employees.

The Digital Worker allows caseloads to continue to be serviced despite the human worker shortage. This allows constituents to still have paperwork processed in a judicious fashion. RPA enhances the system's ability to serve the people, even with a dwindling workforce. The added efficiency and help with reporting that Digital Workers provide could very well be the answer to setting up the future of government jobs. While the goal is not scaling back on employees in the government sector, it may be inevitable. Again, why wait until the problem is at critical mass to start working on the solution?

FEAR THE FUTURE OR LEARN THE FUTURE

In the age of technology, things don't get swept under the rug—they get broadcast as live or recorded videos on social media. This has led to really horrific PR issues between military, police, and first responders around the world. Lanshore looks at the problems and says, "What is our responsibility to this? Do the minds that make up our teams have the capacity to solve real world problems in real time using RPA?" The answer has always seemed to show up, though there is always room for growth and development of all ideas. We're not going to show you the entirety of the ingredients to a cake we're baking, just how relevant and advanced RPA could be in solving issues other than clerical issues.

One of the first ideas Doug threw around was the way people feel with blue lights flashing behind them. No one really gets a warm fuzzy feeling, it's a fast dread that sinks to the bottom of the stomach pretty quickly, "Oh, here we go." RPA would have to learn in the real world how people were responding to officers pulling them over to build a data set that could create data points to help build a spectrum of data points that helped change police interactions overall.

What if traffic stops in an area were tested as not violations based? Blue lights go on, citizen pulls over, cop says, "Hey, just wanted to say you're driving great, here's $50 gift card/free coffees." Person in car is a little annoyed that they were slowed down by the stop, but that was a different interaction. Now, do this thousands of times in a town until the blue lights aren't always negative, unless its necessary. The idea is that RPA removes the racial element. This will get more concrete in a moment. This part was an interesting build up of a social experiment that could help the implementation of the next phase.

To make this clear, this is not a political or opinion piece on the incident we are about to mention. This incident shook the world and is not an isolated event. Sadly, there are incidences between civilians and law enforcement that come under scrutiny of both the public and review boards. The George Floyd incident is what made us start thinking about RPA and the responsibility to innovate and help solve real world problems that may have solutions within our reach that may not be clear to field insiders who have done what they can with the dwindling resources available.

While we are staying away from political points about the issue, we would like to say, the premise while brainstorming these ideas is that human life is precious and unnecessary loss of life is to be avoided. The loss of George Floyd's life set of a domino effect of things that could have been avoided with preventative measures.

On May 25, 2020, there was an incident that brought law enforcement officers to the scene where George Floyd would lose his life. The incident began over a counterfeit bill and an altercation. Neither infraction being serious. The ultimate loss of George's life could have been avoided.

Law enforcement needs help. It's known as the "good ol' boys' club" for a reason with the mentality of having each other's backs because it's required in the toughest streets. The problem is objectivity is hard to reach in an environment where watching out for each other is essential. Someone's bad day gets swept under the rug, and unfortunately, bad days getting swept under the rug too long can have fatal ramifications for the civilians in the path of someone that might have desperately needed a break.

Derek Chauvin had a history of offenses in the field since the 2001 start to his law enforcement career. Out of 18 complaints against Chauvin, only two resulted in disciplinary action. The database had seven complaints of police brutality that ended in no discipline. In 2006, Chauvin was part of five other officers that shot and killed a man for stabbing his girlfriend and another person. In 2008, during an altercation with a domestic dispute, Chauvin shot a man twice, though he survived. In 2011, he and four other officers were put on a three-day leave for shooting an "indigenous man" who also survived but was allowed back to work after the investigation deemed it appropriate force. The other officers involved in Floyd's death have had multiple grievances against them as well.[4]

Questions arise when hearing information like this. Were there any internal audits of the files of officers to do further training or risk assessment before placing them in the field? If so, what were the results? If not, why not? What are the parameters used to make disciplinary or employment decisions? Who audits the database and officer files? Who is to blame for the oversight?

Clearly, over the years, Chauvin had pulled the trigger multiple times. Other than a three-day suspension, what measures were taken? Was he given therapy or counseling? Was he being monitored for PTSD? Shooting someone is a traumatic event. Was he becoming desensitized to street violence? What trainings and community outreach programs were Chauvin a part of to familiarize him with the people he was sworn to protect and serve? There are hundreds more questions we can ask, but we will only take this line of questioning a little further before presenting a possible solution. Was Chauvin racially profiling suspects? Was he prejudiced or racist? Did he measure the offense and record fairly? Where was his empathy and control in the face of a man begging for his life and saying he couldn't breathe?

Understand, we pushed those questions to make a point. Knowing the level of comradery necessary to help a law enforcement group thrive in each other's presence, there must be a counter measure to seniority issues, favoritism, short-staffed oversight, etc. Using a Digital Worker to evaluate and manage what officers might need a break from working the streets might take the stress off the superior officers and the ones working in the field.

Humans are undeniably the most valuable asset to any company. It is important to not cause burnout in employees, especially when lives are at stake. Even inattention to detail could cost an officer, or someone in their path, their life unnecessarily. So, how do we remove the human element while preserving the human spirit in the process?

It's a great question. Lanshore believes that a system that grades certain infractions and lines them up with the proper disciplinary options, where one must be chosen and enacted by the superior officer would change the interaction.

This is a hypothetical situation. For instance, Officer A was too rough in the field last night and the complaint was police brutality. That corresponds to the option 2B, under investigation, where the officer is put on leave for up to 3 days while the situation is investigated. If the claim is found to be invalid, officer comes back, no discipline. If the claim is found to be valid, the Digital Worker pops options for discipline up on the screen that correspond to the local law and rules of the law enforcement agency.

The Digital Worker documents the choice of the superior officer and dictates into the personal file what the ramifications and findings were. This file is held and sent along parameters that are set for the safety of the civilians. Multiple infractions cause the Digital Worker to escalate the issues appropriately up the chain of command without being manually sent. This takes out the possibility of human error or oversight.

The Digital Worker is not going to discriminate based on experiences with humans, race, age, gender, sexual orientation, personality preferences, or any other determining factor that a human might prefer or not. This eliminates the possibility of a least favorite officer receiving harsher punishment or a favorite receiving far less than they should. The Digital Worker would also be able to audit the decisions of the superior officer to make sure that they were not consistently choosing the semi-harsher choice for certain people while choosing the easier path for other people.

The Digital Worker could work on a numerical base and an absolute escalation system as well. The Digital Worker also ensures that in a high stress situation, only the coding needs to go through for emails to start up through the channels. For instance, an officer gets injured, and instead of the superior officer making dozens of calls and trying to get everyone notified that needs notified, they pull the file onto the screen, click a button, and emails start filing out while the superior officer races to check on their officer or go to family, etc. Then someone internally is taking care of media requests, shutting down improper communication channels, deploying more help, if necessary, or whatever other things must be done.

Chapter 7

Digital Doctors and Medical RPA

The medical landscape has changed drastically over the years. Urgent cares, hospitals, individual provider practices, and other medical facilities have been popping up all over the place. Medical care has advanced to extend lives and is available to more people than any time in the past.

Digital workers can help with the many processes that are involved in the different medical buildings across the country and the world. Billing, various reports, scheduling, time management, onboarding/offboarding, and other processes can easily transition to RPA. What other ways can RPA be utilized within the medical world to streamline and help on a daily basis?

DIAGNOSTIC ROBOTS

It is my opinion that a robot would be better than a human in a clinical setting. Machines learn from data collected, while human learn from limited textbooks selected by their professors and on-the-job-training. There are scenarios where a human doctor will be more effective than a human doctor. Let's run the diagnostics.

ROBOT DR. VERSUS DR. DOUG

Let's imagine a Robot Doctor is up against Dr. Doug. An ambulance shows up with a trauma patient bleeding from his ears, unconscious from a car wreck, and EMTs are calling out what they started as treatment en route. In this scenario, Robot Doctor is ill equipped to run diagnostics. Dr. Doug is going to have the advantage correctly assessing the emergency situation and starting tests for brain injuries while continuing managing the bleeding and additional steps needed to pull the patient back from the danger of needing to take time out to answer questions for Robot Doctor. At any point though, Robot Doctor could be brought in to compare captured patient data to information stored from similar traumas and help guide the response of Dr. Doug. If Dr. Doug hasn't dealt with head traumas often, Robot Doctor could help Dr. Doug understand the options and tests available to give the patient the nest chances of a fast and successful recovery.

In non-critical situations, Robot Doctor is going to lead the questioning based on answers to help narrow or extend a search parameter for individual patient's needs. This eliminates the chance that rare diagnoses are misdiagnosed or missed due to any provider's lack of experience with issues they may not have encountered. Another great byproduct of RPA in medicine, more advanced than what is already in use, is getting to the root of issues sooner. Many diagnoses take many visits and further suffering on part of the patient because treatment is based on prioritizing symptoms. RPA can follow through much faster and say, "These are possibilities based on the symptoms the patient is explaining. Ask these questions... Here are the tests to look for these possible health issues... When the results come in, we will be able to look into this further."

Imagine treating a Vitamin D deficiency which causes lethargy etc. with something that causes Vitamin D deficiency. That's an example and we aren't here to give medical advice, just show that inviting RPA to help doctors increase their care of patients ends up being a win-win for the doctor and the patient.

Medical malpractice suits cause doctors a lot of issues financially. As of 2016, it was reported by John Hopkins that medical errors were the third leading cause of death with an estimated 250,000 deaths each year.[1] Dr, Michael Makary, who led the study, talked to media and said that reporting needed to change on death certificates, but changes hadn't been made. The doctor defines death due to medical error in multiple ways: inadequately skilled staff available during care, error in judgment of care, a system issue (computer issues, dosage or types of medications given errors), or a preventable adverse effect to medicine or complications from surgeries that aren't recorded.[2] A story was shared about a hospital overdose due to not enough employees and a backlog of doctor's orders in the pharmacy that caused a mix-up in medication then administered by a nurse. The point made was it was an avoidable issue, and the article admits new tools will help change the game. How can these issues be managed?

The computer systems should be run with RPA, completely connected and prioritizing tasks for human workers. The Digital Worker would have coded within the program different levels of need and urgency. An emergency order would rise to the top—for example, an intravenous anticoagulant might be imperative for a blood clot patient, respiratory issues, things like that would jump above pill form pain relievers and antacids. The doctors could also mark medications urgent so the pharmacists could ensure the most pressing issues were being dealt with immediately. The Digital Worker could also have a double check option, where it reminded the pharmacist to double check the dosage and medication. Their click in that box would put the responsibility squarely on them making them more aware of what was going to the patient.

There are layers to explore, the medication gets scanned in by nurses, and the Digital Worker could prompt the nurse to double check what they are administering, taking that extra moment to not just administer but to also check the packaging.

RPA systems have the ability to tie to other systems, so doctors could opt in to giving access to medical records to local hospitals for a pathway to charts for patients needing immediate care or scheduled for surgeries. Patients would agree to this at the doctor's office, and it could aid in crosschecking prescriptions if a patient is brought in unconscious through emergency or didn't remember to update current medications before a surgery, etc. This could cut down on repetitive testing and additional tests ordered to find a problem with a patient would also be shared directly on the patient's chart, so the doctor sees additional workups and results. There could also be fail safes within the Digital Worker that alerts any lags in the system or computer errors.

Doctors and nurses already put a lot of notes in the system, so a Digital Worker that has been coded to find anomalies in reports or alert when there could be contraindications with medications could make a big difference. The Digital Worker would be able to search online for more information quicker as boxes are checked and alert the doctor to supplementary tests and possibilities.

What do these errors cost? Is there a ROI, not that you can put a price on a human life? What is medical malpractice costing the industry? In 2018, the National Practitioner Data Bank reported $4,031,987,700 in payouts. The average payout was $348,065 per malpractice case. Diagnosis was the leading reason for malpractice payouts at 34.1% of malpractice allegations followed by surgery and treatment.[3] Over $4 billion dollars not including lawyer fees and other costs associated with litigation and loss of time, reputation, and added stress.

Robot Doctors could help cut down the risk by being able to compare data to other online systems and quickly finding possibilities to help the doctor choose tests and diagnoses, and it would be interesting to see a discount in insurance rates in the future for doctors that use RPA as part of their practice, much like homeowners enjoy risk assessment breaks in premium for having security systems and fire alarms. When technology starts changing industries, there is a cost-savings that can be assessed against years prior. The goal is always growing capabilities while lowering risks.

Managing the time exhaustive work in offices and establishments matches the business world—calendars, merging files, sharing files with other systems, scheduling, billing, accounting, HR management, etc.

Chapter 8

Ethical Tech and Tech Challenges

Advances in technology raise interesting questions around the table. What if robots take over the world and enslave humanity? We aren't going that far in this chapter, but we will look at the ethical questions facing automation and the challenges that arise out of the concerns.

LOSING THE HUMAN TOUCH

One of the ways tech companies plug RPA is to reduce headcount. While that could be a reality when a Digital Worker is managing copious amounts of swivel-chair tasks, the ultimate goal is to optimize the customer experience. The byproduct may be reducing hours spent on mundane tasks which may eliminate headcount and the company may make more money. Many companies don't reduce headcount, they refocus the talent in their staff to more satisfying tasks which increases productivity and job satisfaction. Using RPA correctly can be a win-win for everyone involved.

When is the last time you called a business and talked to a human? People remark on calling anywhere and being met by automated answering services, having to navigate lengthy messages with instructions to pick a number and hope that a human ends up on the phone at some point. Call the IRS and try to get a human on the line. During tax season, it isn't uncommon that every option leads to a dump zone where there is a message instructing the caller to check statuses online. Why? There just aren't enough call centers to handle millions of calls during tax season. Creating that many temporary jobs and training that many people wouldn't be an effective strategy when most people can find out their filing or refund status and the answers to frequently asked questions through the online prompts.

People are tired of robots; they just want to talk to someone who can fix their problem. Utilizing RPA successfully frees up human capital to get a person adequately in front of the customers to make them happy. Someone calling in to get a balance or bill amount or to pay quickly will navigate the prompts to get off the call and some prefer this. Having the options available considerably lowers the chance that a customer is errantly bounced to a hundred different associates, repeating their concerns, getting frustrated, and the worst, having their call dropped after they've been bounced around trying to get someone competent on the phone. Intelligent automation is expedience of service.

Many businesses handling large geographical areas of clients also employ automated answering options to handle the number of calls that come in. Susie can only answer so many calls asking what someone owes and processing payments, but an automated system can handle more with more security for the customer. Instead of repeating numbers over and over, you use the phone or your voice, press the pound button and easily move through the prompts. Call over, no awkward silences or uncomfortable misunderstandings. This frees Susie up to handle her clerical duties or other tasks and handle people with concerns outside of what an automated system can handle. While this may frustrate customers that like the human touch for all interactions, most people are fine with employing the automated option and being done.

The human touch is enhanced by automation when considering job satisfaction of employees and not leaving dozens of people in queue, "You are the twenty-second caller in line. The wait time is currently expected to be fifty-eight minutes." We all have better things to do than wait on hold, although sometimes its necessary. An employee that isn't exasperated by being on monotonous calls for entire shifts will treat the people they encounter with more patience, for the most part, and handle their concerns in a less rushed fashion. Obviously, this is being handled at a basic level.

The best answer is humans will never be fully removed. Robots can do a lot of things. We're focused on automated processes in this book, but there are robots milking cows, closing boxes and sending them down shipping lanes, building cars, stamping steel, filling bottles, etc. People are still used in each instance.

Milking cows—a farmer and other farmhands corral the cows into the milking area, ready the cows with iodine and place the machinery on the udders, watch the process while repeatedly moving through the herd down the line. They will also check the milk tanks, hook hoses to milk trucks, possibly test quality/cleanliness, and someone has to start the cleaning process of the machines and milking area when finished. Amazon builds incredible fulfilment centers for orders. Humans and robots work together to pick orders, box them, and send them to the right truck. They couldn't fulfill the number of orders that floods in every day. According to 2019 statistics, Amazon ships approximately 1.6 million packages every day. The math on that is more than 66,000 orders every hour or eighteen and a half orders per second.[1] Removing automated processes from the equation (printing labels and order sheets, boxes being ready and available, shipping material to protect products, the shipping robot that reads labels and pushes them to the right truck, etc.) would make this large of an operation much more difficult, or maybe impossible. Growth requires out-of-the-box solutions.

The problem becomes less human touch when we consider businesses in areas where employees are hard to find and where unemployment is low. It is great when there is a surplus of available jobs, but it doesn't help businesses in need of employees when there aren't people lining up with resumes and applications. Automating with RPA changes the swivel chair work (repetitive tasks that require multiple screens) by allowing the Digital Worker to manage rule-based functions. Now, an automated company can hire for more exciting roles, allowing them to attract individuals who know they want more from a career than punching numbers from one place to the next. Without automation, some companies may continue excessive turnover and not attract the best forward-thinking minds to their companies.

The Millennials, and the generations after them, are growing up alongside technology. The future belongs to them, and they are more technologically advanced than workers in the past. To attract them to companies, automation of repetitive, time-consuming, mind numbingly mundane work will be necessary. Companies that don't automate might terminate or only serve their local community (small scale). An example of this might be a small bakery or a local thrift shop, neither of which may need to automate to continue in their market. Companies that want to grow outside of the local market will see automation being their competitive edge or their lack of automation will become a stumbling block.

CROSSING THE TRAIN LINE-LET'S TALK UNION

Humans in business is also a concern for unions that protect jobs for the union members. Automating jobs has made certain tasks at factories more efficient and safer for the workers. Robots taking over the bulk of the process in some manufacturing facilities has happened, where far less employees are necessary. The unions will get on board with automation as long as the jobs of the members they protect aren't threatened.

Even more than that, there are certain places that could be automated, but won't or shouldn't be. The human touch is irreplaceable by machines in certain parts of society.

The train lines are a big thing in Germany and the UK. Automation could be lined up to free up having an employee at abeyance bridges, but the human touch of the wave and the knowledge that there is a human there is important to people. Nostalgia and the safety citizens feel when there is a person strategically placed can outweigh the benefits of automation. Certain historically important human placements will not be replaced.

An amazing example universally is airplane pilots. The commercial planes fly themselves to the setting. Small plane pilots have to work harder than pilots in commercial jets. One single jet plane pilot told me recently that he invited his brother, who is a commercial pilot, to fly his plane and his brother admitted he has forgotten how to fly a plane. The commercial pilot is there to fly or land the plane should any of the instruments fail and the control system get knocked out. William Langewiesche tackled this in an article in the *New York Times*.[2] He spoke about the safety implications of a declining level of aircraft systems knowledge among new pilots. The article addressed airlines meeting the growing demand for pilots by reducing the experience qualifications for employment. New pilots are left handling failed or partially failed systems without proper training because it is a secondary concern when it comes to selecting new hires. The result is a deep understanding of aircraft systems operation is becoming a less common trait among pilots. This is problematic because the automation in the airplanes is so advanced making training subpar without experience with the different problems that can arise.

Automation should never take over the competency of the operator. This is where automation fails.

The train line human is at his or her post more for nostalgia than necessity. There are systems that can be tripped by a moving train, as seen in the US at crossings. The pilot though must be capable and fully trained despite planes being automated to the hilt. This is an example of the polarities found within the technological world.

WORLD DOMINATION

Now that we have your attention, RPA is not AI. Let me repeat that: Robotic Processes Automation is not Artificial Intelligence. Could it be merged someday? Most likely, but RPA is rule-based and controlled by human parameters. RPA uses little to no AI.

AI is widely misunderstood. As we stumble more and more into it, we learn its limitations and what goes into training it. Of course, there will be entire tomes on it, and there already are, but we'll touch on it here. You can tell a person you live in Texas, and if you give them an address in Maine, they might look at you funny and remind you mentioned living in Texas. If you tell AI you live in Maine, even though you live in Texas, it stores Maine. AI can defer decisions, like "this is a bad person." It might take thousands upon thousands of graphical representations of Osama bin Laden before AI says, "With 99.9876% certainty, that is Osama bin Laden." You could slip a picture in that AI has never encountered and it might not recognize him, whereas a human would most likely know who he was, without having seen a particular picture before.

AI learns from pictures. Imagine AI seeing hundreds of pictures of a flux capacitor. AI learns the flex capacitor, but it hasn't become a reality yet, while AI would see it as concretely existing based on what it has encountered of it—pictures, diagrams, movie stills, etc. Obviously, AI can't dominate the world when the humans are teaching it with materials available to us. Will AI continue to evolve? Of course, and we will touch on how it will grow leaps in bounds in a second.

BAD DATA AS A CAREER OPTION

Imagine companies advertising this career: "Errant Data Creator," or something to that effect. As AI evolves in business, it will do competitor research to help companies advance their products and services. AI works by learning from what is available. So, people start creating fake websites on a massive scale, running up (or down) pricing information and sale data, leaving AI research to run analyses and reports that have skewed information forcing AI reliant companies making decisions based on bad data. The internet already houses plenty of invalid information.

This possibility would make small and large businesses engage in a covert war. A small business could figure out what their large competitors were scanning and corrupt the data by investing in a bad data creator instead of advertising and increasing the value of their products or service. Likewise, a large company could cripple a small business quite easily this way, if the small company relied heavily on bad data to make decisions. The business committed to leveraging technology to learn would manipulate algorithms and data to their advantage.

Corporate espionage using data to hurt competitor's ability to make decisions would be on a level we haven't seen yet, and it exists but not to the scale it could in the future. Another thing that AI could learn within a company is when a problem occurs with data inside the company if someone slipped incorrect data into the system. A human might miss mistakes in data because we would have to know whether the data was wrong or right. If twenty percent of the data was wrong, now we have to figure out what went wrong, where, and why. Once we know all of that, a human can fix it. AI can scan multiple audit reports (as can RPA), and AI can make changes (RPA cannot), so this is another thing imperative to consider while programming.

SATURATION POINTS

When a product or service has been maximized in the marketplace, we say it has reached its saturation point. Some concerns for tech companies in this space is RPA will eventually reach this point. That's rubbish. Improving upon and finding new uses for products or services within the market keeps this from happening. We could say that cell phones have reached the saturation point because most everyone that can afford or wants one has one. The trend is the cell phone makers coming out with updated and new models, different colors, upgrades for users that have older models, etc. There hasn't been a moment in the market where cell phone companies threw up their hands and said, "By George, we will never sell another cell phone, we have reached the saturation point and can go no further."

Advancing technologies won't do that either. Whether a company starts with one Digital Worker or five, as they grow and see the value of automating processes, get a fuller picture of the return on investment, they are going to want to add to their cadre of Digital Workers to free up human capital. The unspoken fear is that Digital Workers will replace humans, and there will be some of that. When turnover rates threaten budgets due to consistently training new employees, jobs that are repetitive and can be handled by a Digital Worker will be. The ROI, or trade off, is funds can be used towards marketing products and services which can create more jobs in other areas of the company, whether they need to hire more salespeople, repair people, factory workers, customer service reps, etc. Companies may find that Digital Workers save them money on processes that were throwing human resources down the drain and could start multiple new locations, which also creates numerous jobs across the board.

There will never be a moment with RPA where the saturation point is hit and there are no new opportunities. Just like we have pointed out earlier, innovation and creation of new ways to utilize RPA may come about. That's encouraging with

RPA as a future field for generations that are coming out of high school knowing how to code and maximize their success with technology. It is more likely that unprecedented opportunities will arise as the creators of tomorrow arrive on the scene and tinker with what tech giants have started.

ETHICAL AGREEMENTS

Naturally, it is idealistic to theorize that scientists and data scientists could and would sign ethical agreements. The truth of the matter is there will always be someone with malicious intent and no conscious to keep them from misusing AI. We can see throughout history how things that should have been used for the greater good was weaponized.

Coming up with an ethical agreement poses its own glitches. How do you define ethical or unethical use of AI? Who is creating the definitions? Some people think eliminating millions of people is good for the earth while others believe that eliminating humans is unethical. The conclusions reached by different individuals about what is right deciding the correct way to use technology sounds like a dangerous judgment to make.

If a consortium of people go rogue we end up with what is being discussed on the world stage right now with censorship encroaching on free speech globally through social media platforms. Censors are becoming thought police and silencing topics, banning people from various platforms, and have shown that they have the power to shut off people that think differently from the people making the decisions to censor opposing thoughts, beliefs, opinions, information. This creates an environment where people have to figure out how to exist within the boundaries of their opponents or find themselves deplatformed. While this is a serious ethical concern and issue, it is small potatoes compared to what could arise in the future. That isn't the topic of this book, but it will be its own area of study someday.

MOORE'S LAW AND QUANTUM PROCESSING

These are interesting topics that deserve to be mentioned, if for no other reason than to open minds to the vast topics within technology.

Moore's Law states that computer processing should double every few years. It is the opinion within the tech world that Moore's Law is coming to an end. Gordon Moore, one of the cofounders of Intel speculated that the trend for fitting more transistors in the same space and the belief was the trend would continue and change technology exponentially, and that has been true since the 1970's until (there's a debate on when), but Moore's Law is being treated like it's dead now. Intel disclosed they were slowing the pace launching new chip-making technology. The gap between successive generations will widen. "The transistors in Intel's latest chips already have features as small as 14 nanometers, and it is becoming more difficult to shrink them further in a way that's cost-effective for production."[3] As chip sizes close in on subatomic levels of silicon, there comes a point where we've maxed out power with the shrinking size.

Some people will argue that this slows down technology, but it isn't exactly true. As it pertains to RPA and AI, the importance of Moore's Law is speed to decision. For instance, if Moore's Law is used to predict when generalized AI will make a decision with accuracy, and we know this year it takes ten minutes for computation, we can expect the same computation to take five minutes in two years, and 2.5 minutes in another two years. According to Moore's Law, we would expect processes to take half the time in two years, so we would program and plan around those numbers. That doesn't seem to be a big deal until think what Moore's Law would mean to a company that needs 40,000 of those same computations DAILY. You can increase ability by two or decrease cost by two. A computer's operating ability and speed of function can be increased with faster and up-to-date hardware. If any given program takes five minutes to load and operate, RPA can't speed up the hardware operating time, just the rate at which it runs through the information will be faster than a human opening everything and making comparisons, for example. Loading RPA onto slower equipment doesn't give the advantage.

Let's look at this another way, can you walk and chew gum at the same time? Most likely. A computer can be programmed to run huge calculus problems, but to program it to make coffee, pour it in a cup with cream and sugar to your liking, answer the door for someone it's never met before, and other tasks we deal with daily, is too much.

AI is generalized intelligence. It has the processing power to do what the human brain can and complete multiple tasks at a time. BUT it would take thousands of computers to do what a human being does logically and easily every day. A human can wake up, start coffee, change the clothes over, get multiple children ready for their days, answer calls, emails, messages, sign papers, prepare meals, run errands, and more. Humans were managing these various tasks before automation and can handle it all without electronic help, although it all gets easier with technology.

Hardware is what is susceptible to Moore's Law. It's hard to get smaller than technology already is and gain net increases in speed or hardware function. Processing then has to take on a new format to make sense. This leads into quantum processing. Different technology requires a different way of managing the binary or the reading of electrical impulses. Quantum processing is that much greater and faster that 256-bit encryption can be cracked in about 8 hours with what is currently available (depending on who does the math and the qubits), but I suspect it will get faster as the computers learn. Right now, they believe it would take billions of years to crack 256-bit encryption with normal operating systems.

Quantum processing is where we may see AI take a massive leap forward. There are tech giants with quantum processors and the facilities are humongous. It isn't feasible to make the quantum processing smaller yet because of cooling issues.

While researching this book, there was information on a Chinese company offering a "quantum computer" out in the fourth quarter (right after publishing date) and it sounded impressive until the specs. The next smallest unit is 121 pounds, so we will stand by it is going to take time to figure out how to be as amazing in less space when it comes to quantum computing. The monster desktop is relatively cheap for a quantum computer but will set you back $50,000 compared to ten-million-dollar commercial quantum processors.[4] These options are interesting yet as fast as the tech world changes could be rendered obsolete in a few years. Its better to invest in something that is functional and can be changed to accommodate the needs and expectations of companies (like Digital Workers).

Chapter 9

Automating Post Covid

"Our future is a race between the growing power of our technology and the wisdom with which we use it. Let's make sure wisdom wins."
Stephen Hawking

The work landscape changed amid the global pandemic of 2020. With non-essential businesses closing their doors to accommodate mandates, businesses either had to adapt or they realized that the way they did business wasn't sustainable as they were in mitigating circumstances. Small businesses took a hit during lockdowns and many closed. This was unavoidable for some businesses. RPA would not have made a difference for a mom-and-pop sit down restaurant that couldn't open with employees.

The picture painted by the Finance and Economics Discussion Series, Divisions of Research & Statistics and Monetary Affairs of the Federal Reserve Board is dire: "Our sector-level results suggest economywide excess establishment exit—that is, exit above and beyond pre-pandemic rates—was likely below 200,000 establishments during the first year of the pandemic, implying an exit rate about one-quarter to one-third above normal."[1] The official numbers won't be available until later, and business exit (death) are expected, but this excess of almost 200,000 business deaths is above the normal rate, which is 400,000 business deaths annually.

Alarming headlines like "9 million U.S. small businesses fear they won't survive pandemic"[2] became commonplace. People watched helplessly as businesses sold off assets and closed their doors permanently. Some of you may have been affected personally and are struggling to thrive or are starting over.

RPA can make the difference—pandemic or no pandemic, the lesson is clear: Cost saving efforts that maximize work output are necessary to success in business. In the event that employees need time off for quarantine or family needs in the future, are all measures within the company maximized so one missing employee doesn't tank the whole operation? It's time to begin planning business in a way that makes business sustainable with a skeleton crew.

Companies have contingency plans in place for normal short-term catastrophes, but a global pandemic would have been hard to plan for, given how quickly things changed from "we're keeping an eye on this" to "two weeks to slow the curve." The two weeks turned to months, and it became clear that adaptability to a new way of life was the only way for companies to survive. Interesting conversations revolving around RPA came out of the race to change the way work was done. Remote work became a way for companies to continue serving their clientele while dealing with lockdown or closure rules as well as parents that now had children doing schoolwork from home with no childcare.

RPA became a measure of sustainability. UiPath, one of the leaders in RPA, worth $35 Billion dollars on the market (as of the writing of this book), did a study discovering that "66% of employees said RPA enables them to have more human interactions because of how it restructures their work."[3] This is relevant to the changing landscape of the workplace because human interaction between customers and clients with employees builds a rapport that is missing in an office setting. Having employees focus primarily on mundane tasks like data entry from home doesn't maximize the skillsets and meet the needs of clientele that can use Google to find another business online competing in your space. The Digital Worker can build reports and data spreads so employees can use video chats and old-fashioned phone calls to connect with customers.

Companies didn't have a long-term plan to maintain prolonged remote work, but automation empowers the reality. Automation permits companies to move forward with their digital transformation initiatives while employees continue working from home. Organizations can capitalize post Covid by transforming into dexterous, full RPA enterprises, even with the workforce outside the office. Tech departments are able to create pathways into legacy programs that enable remote workers to continue their jobs without overhauling entire systems or risking data breaches or losses by changing systems. The cost savings and added security that the Digital Worker can provide could be invaluable long-term, but there isn't a good way of fully measuring what expensive headaches were missed because of good decision making and the right team handling the automation switch-over. What would a loss of data, changing and retraining systems, or losing entire departments of employees with no way to execute tasks remotely cost a company? The time figuring out possible losses or costs associated with bad data management and the inability to operate certain departments within an organization could be better spent making a plan that includes automating efficiently.

As Lanshore execs writing this book, it's hard not to get excited about the vision we have been working on for years now getting the attention we know it deserves. Let us share some projections that show we aren't just speaking from our love for robotic automation of processes, although it is exciting to imagine all the ways RPA can play out in the future. "'It's tough to compare this to any other industry,' says Bryan Bergin, an analyst at Cowen. 'It's a market that's showing dramatic adoption.'"[4] Forrester estimates that in 2022, our market will reach revenue of $2.9 Billion dollars, which is a ten-fold increase from 2016 numbers. The projected AI office market for 2022 is $48.5 Billion.[4] While there are a lot of factors that go into the projections, such as bill-pay, RPA, and other bots doing work within fields, these are big numbers.

Now, imagine, as big as these numbers are, these Digital Workers cost a fraction of a salary and can be maintained for years. This doesn't mean companies have to get rid of their employees, but they may not need to hire and train large turnover positions which saves time and human capital all around. In a post Covid economic situation, any way to save money and redefine the way the company operates can give an organization the edge on competitors. Lean operating options like RPA beat dumping more work on a few employees who could find offers elsewhere as companies look to replace workers. Digital Workers may be the way to attract talent to a company because the monotonous work is managed, and new hires can look forward to minimal clean-up of files while focusing on what gets them excited about your company.

The post Covid world has seen many companies fail, it's true. Displaced workers have options and will go where they see the most opportunity for growth and less stress. Until unemployment rates reach pre-pandemic numbers, competitive companies will be able to recruit the workers that bring the most to their organization.

Do you want to be placing a recurring ad for "data entry" or "visionary management position?" Organizations need to take responsibility for the bars we set for our teams. If we consistently hire low-level jobs with low-level titles, we can't feel let down when the employee punches the clock in and out and doesn't care about the overall wellbeing of the company. The culture isn't there. Post Covid restructuring with Digital Workers may help redesign the workplace. Digital Workers don't ever say things like, "You don't pay me enough to care." They just deliver the reports, data, and info in their rule base. Creating a place where the staff comes in with an attitude of gratitude and ready to face a day of something other than repetitive work can change more than just the bottom line. For the companies trying to find the silver lining in the pandemic, changing the entire mindset of the company can be done effectively with Digital Workers. Get the vision and deliver it (See Chapter 12 for inspiration).

The Post-Covid era should be seen as an opportunity for advancement of technology within organizations. Now, it is clear how quickly things can change when a global issue breeches the monotony of daily routine. Can organizations survive annual lockdowns for illness if it would become a reoccurring thing on the global landscape? How do we brace for the possibility there is one more or ongoing lockdowns? Digitization of the workforce is one way, and RPA makes the most sense since it optimizes employees already employed but can keep vital reports and information moving. It can also connect remote workers should employees need to work from home in a manageable way. It's time to start making changes that enhance possibilities of future success. It does not behoove anyone for companies to fail due to lack of planning.

Chapter 10

Global Adoption

The only boundaries that RPA knows are adoption rates. RPA can advance most every industry: government processes, the medical field, education at all levels, businesses, both small and large. The only barrier would be lack of computers or electronic devices in general. In other words, we do not expect Amazonian tribes to adopt new technologies.

Let's look at the outlook for RPA globally. As of 2018, North America leads the world in adopting Digital Workers and corners the market by 41%. This isn't surprising to anyone in the tech world. What it means is: The rest of the world has some catching up to do. Western Europe comes in next at 28% followed by China at 22% of market revenue share worldwide.

The United States is unlikely to lag behind anytime soon, which is both good and bad news. The bad news is that US based companies will be more competitive as they begin and continue to eliminate and improve on processes using human capital, while utilizing Digital Workers wherever possible to widen the profit margin. As RPA advances, the gap could widen on the world stage, unless other countries become educated on the value of having Digital Workers and start adopting them at higher rates.

Robotic Process Automation (RPA) Market Revenue Share Worldwide in 2018, by region

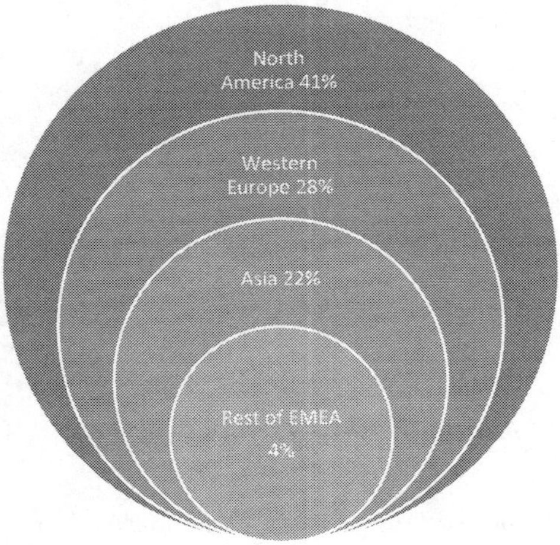

According to Brandessence Market Research and Consulting, "The global demand for global robotic process automation (RPA) market size in terms of revenue was worth of USD 2715.75 Million in 20-20 and is expected to reach USD 18339.95 Million in 2027…"[1] That's a growth rate of over 31%, which is huge considering we're already talking large numbers.

LET'S TALK STATS

Deloitte conducted a global survey in September 2017 of 400 individuals representing organizations with a collective worth of $1.8 Trillion. According to the results of the survey, 53% had begun their RPA excursion. The projection was for 72% to begin within two years of the survey, which set a pace for near global adoption in five years.

Companies were reporting the use of a digital workforce was paying them back within 12 months with the Digital Workers averaging 20% of the full-time equivalent (FTE).

When it came to Digital Workers meeting or exceeding expectations: 92% of the 400 were reporting improved compliance; 90% reported improved accuracy and quality; 86% noted improved productivity; and 59% recorded significant cost reductions. Looking at all the upsides to Digital Workers had 78% planning to increase their investment in RPA within their organizations over the next three years, while also admitting that only 3% had scaled their digital workforce.[1] Successfully helping companies scale the way they operate with Digital Workers is something Lanshore likes to do, but we also want to see the barriers to adoption, globally, fall to the ground so business becomes more competitive.

ROYAL REPORT—RPA IN THE UK

Deloitte did a UK specific study on technology's impact on jobs. The findings are incredible! Over the last 20 years, technology has eliminated 800,000 jobs. That sounds like a lot until you reach their next finding that applied technology has theoretically helped in the creation of 3.5 million higher cognition jobs that pay more than 10 thousand pounds more per year. That is the equivalent of almost $14,000 when compared to the dollar. This has created an estimated 140 billion pounds in new earnings in the UK economy, across all regions, which is a huge increase and testament to the benefits of automation. Deloitte is calling this the shift "from brawn to brains."[2]

The study goes on to discuss that automation is making way for more creativity and the need for skills that graduate level humans embody. This starts a cycle of a more educated population to fill higher paying jobs. These employees would be career minded and trained, as well as educated, so the job market would become more competitive and drive more people into universities to get their educations to fill job openings as they graduate. Success has a way of creating a winning cycle. Companies will have to show up with better benefits and job offers to get the best minds while other cultivated minds are gaining experience making them more competitive and willing to leave a job for work that is meaningful to them.

Deloitte also found that half of the jobs in London couldn't benefit from more RPA yet, as they were higher cognition jobs, while other areas of the UK could greatly benefit from updating their processes wit Digital Workers. Large cities and money centers tend to have more automation that has given way to higher cognitive, higher paying careers that allow the Digital Workers to run their task-oriented work so the focus can be on innovation and building business relationship.

The UK survey was very positive towards automation; and interestingly, while businesses were planning to automate more in the future, they had plans to hire more people as well. Organizations, educators, businesses, and policymakers will have to work together to continue the success that Digital Workers can drive. Future job requirements will continue to change with technological advances. The UK has seen incredible leaps and bounds with the adoption of RPA, but there is still a lot of opportunity for more Digital Workers.

According to another Deloitte report, "Organizations that have succeeded in scaling RPA tend to have engaged people and have effectively built buy-in to the change process. In contrast with outsourcing, there seems to be little resistance across organizations to the introduction of RPA."[3] Training current employees to use RPA or asking them to get excited about the Digital Worker taking over mundane tasks will be significantly easier than asking employees to train their replacements or let them know you're shifting their work to someone else.

Employees are still the key to success. Their willingness and ability to scale up with the Digital Workers will make the difference for organizations. This is another place education and continuing education within fields can help foster growth hand in hand with what is coming in the future with organizations. The Digital Workers can execute their tasks, but they can't make the humans read the reports, update them, add the information necessary to move forward at critical junctures where the bot can go no further without information being added or corrected.

Chapter 11

Rolling In with RPA

The next question is going to inflict fear in most hearts: What are you going to automate? That's a huge question, and some minds will go blank. It seems like a huge endeavor.

The best way to get started is by understanding what you do now that makes your organization successful and start defining the steps that your employees take each day. Look at your key employees and think about what would happen if someone quit on the spot. What are the processes they execute and the responsibilities they have? What pieces of the organizational puzzle would suffer without the work done by this person? If one person walking off their job or not being able to work again could cause that many problems, let's escalate this consideration. Now, think about a group or department of employees: What if they were all quarantined? Would the company come to a screeching halt while they got well? Start thinking about the way they go about their jobs, and the individual pieces that allow the company to be successful. Does one process payroll, payable, receivable? Does another reconcile bank statements with the business ledger? It is important to identify as many of the processes as you can. You have a bigger problem if you can't wrap your head around who does what or what departments are managing.

Draw up a day in the life of the company. Start by documenting these processes in as much detail as you can, creating process diagrams. If you need to get a clearer picture by meeting with heads of departments, schedule that. Automating successfully is about having the big picture and doing what makes sense. The gold is in the process definition and enhancement.

Look at each process and determine if it's still necessary; from there, you can fix or change what's already in place. Initially, it makes sense to take the status quo and create the RPA for that, with little to no redefinition. That's where outside eyes and consultants can help make a big difference in the way RPA is implemented early on:

Lanshore's approach is simple: USP.

- Understand the process.
- Select the best tools for the job.
- Proven, repeatable delivery.

The ultimate goal for every client is performance enhancement through optimized operational processes. We help you reach your current and future organizational goals, improving speed, accuracy, efficiency, scalability, responsiveness and cost-effectiveness to support your core business strategy.

SCENE-SETTING & ORGANIZATIONAL EDUCATION

A crucial step is educating key organizational stakeholders on what Robotic Process Automation is and what it can do for them. People may start with a wide range of expectations: from not knowing anything to thinking they can get rid of their entire staff. Often the most useful step, at this stage, is to demonstrate a Digital Worker in action. Buy-in from key players and a top down or bottom-up approach must be decided upon. If the top of the company is a handful of dinosaurs who still write everything, they might not be the ones to get on board. The workers benefitted most might be entry to mid-level employees, but if they are all excited about adopting RPA as part of their daily routine, it may help make the investment make sense. Implementing RPA isn't about making everybody unemployed. UiPath, a well-known RPA vendor, uses the slogan " We make software robots, so people don't have to be robots."

Companies that don't start their business model with RPA have to transition. It isn't always difficult, but it requires having employees that will adopt the technology. There are things that can run and ask for information from the employee that can fill in the fields.

CHOOSING PROCESSES TO AUTOMATE

All investments into technology for a company are looking for ROI (Return on Investment). Government has different goals, but the benefits of Digital Workers make sense across the board. Processes that are highly repetitive and time-consuming make sense to automate. When considering repetitiveness, frequency, complexity, standardization, and supporting documentation, scoring very repetitive or remarkably high frequency processes as the best candidates for RPA.

An additional question to ask to determine which processes offer the best return on investment is the value of the time of the person who's currently executing the manual process. If your managers are caught up in mundane tasks, they are better utilized advancing their departments and overseeing the things being done by the people in their charge. Even an hourly wage entry employee can be saved the headache of mundane tasks and turn their attention to your customers, finding more job satisfaction and possibly better retention rates.

Once you've chosen the best process to automate, the next exercise is to capture screen shots of each step in the process. Those screen shots are then passed to the development and process definition team.

Once the development team is working with the process, they will consider two main questions: the first is to look at the process and ask: "Can we re-architect this process, to make it more streamlined and more effective?"; the second is to consider how best to develop the automated process, so as to ensure that it remains robust, even if the systems change or something minor changes about the process.

If this is the first time a business has worked with process automation, the development of the process may be followed by a proof-of-concept stage, to determine the actual return on investment. Once the business leaders have understood and accepted the benefits of RPA, the need for the proof-of-concept step is reduced. After that, further processes would move from development to testing and then into production.

WHAT RPA MEANS FOR YOUR BUSINESS

Deloitte shows the benefit by asking the companies that have already employed RPA: "More than 90 per cent of organizations surveyed (who have implemented or are scaling robotics) believe that RPA has met or exceeded their expectations on improved productivity, improved compliance and cost to implement."[1]

BENEFITS OF RPA

RPA can automate multi-step, high volume computerized HR, compensation and SPM processes to save time and overheads. A robotic workforce can help reduce costs, increase quality, deliver greater value and a better experience for employees. RPA is already proven and embedded in industries like financial services, insurance and manufacturing.

In HR and compensation, deploying RPA:

- Allows HR employees to focus on higher value work.
- Increases overall employee satisfaction through better, faster service across pay and HR interactions.
- Reduces human error, while gaining consistency and efficiency by automating repetitive tasks.
- Increases operational speed and scalability by using bots to complete tasks within seconds.

• Decreases development costs by enabling business users to create bots with limited IT assistance.

"By 2020, 90% of large and midsize organizations will have at least one process supported by RPA," according to Gartner.[2]

DEVELOPING THE AUTOMATED PROCESS

Assessing current business processes and choosing what to automate is the first step on the road to adding Digital Workers to your organization. This step can seem overwhelming without a firm grasp of how RPA works or what it's capable of. We are including a copy of the Lanshore Process Definition Document at the end of the book, detailing the development side of RPA that can be used as a guideline for planning. It is wise to bring in experts in the early stages of RPA planning, so money isn't wasted automating the wrong processes. Maximizing reward and return on investment might cost more upfront with a consulting agency, like Lanshore, but the headaches and mistakes that are saved in the long run outweigh the start-up costs.

Once the first process to be automated has been chosen, the next step is for the development team to understand the technologies that underlie the manual process. Without getting into the different coding intricacies and issues, which would make sense to coding professionals, but is its own language, it is necessary to understand that successful Digital Workers aren't just available at the snap of a finger. They have to be coded to work with the information and programs your organization uses and requires for success. This is not the place to skimp on attention to detail, because the Digital Worker is rule-based, and the wrong input will mess up the output.

Step 1 – Identify All the Elements You Need. The first step is to identify each different application that is used as part of the process. Examples of different applications to look for and identify could include webpages, database systems, Excel spreadsheets, Word documents, other systems that need to speak to share and audit information, etc. For each different application, you then need to establish and identify all the elements that you need from that application. Once each element has been identified, you need to make sure that you can establish a robust connection to it. Identify everything that the employee would have clicked on, would have copied, would have cross-referenced, would have typed in—the entire procedure they would use to execute their tasks. And, once you've identified the pieces and parts, make sure that each one can be accessed reliably by the RPA tool.

Step 2 – Define the Workflow. Once all the elements are identified and tested, the next step is to begin defining the workflow. The first step in the workflow is to log on to each system. Even at this early stage, you need to be thinking about the exceptions. What happens when something goes wrong, or a pop-up screen interrupts the process? How will the Digital Worker manage the 'Click here if you aren't a robot' prompt? What happens if the login screen doesn't load? You try again, but you also define a timer, to ensure the process can't hang indefinitely. Say, for example, that the log on workflow should take 10 seconds and, after you log into the application, a specific element becomes visible. If you can't identify that element after 10 seconds, you execute the master shutdown and then try again. If you try unsuccessfully three times, you fail the process and send a message that a person needs to investigate.

At every stage you need to be thinking about ways the process might fail and putting in place the necessary exception handling. This goes hand in hand with developing the "happy path", which is the path the process will follow when everything works as expected. As an example, consider a cable TV company that needs to process emails from customers. There are several possible reasons for the emails: one would be the customer writing to change their bank or credit card details; another would be the customer cancelling their cable TV contract. So, based on the contents of the input email, the workflow would need to take one of several different paths.

The development process would get the more straightforward paths working first, and then gradually add paths to deal with more and more of the exceptions. It's unlikely that a workflow would ever succeed in automating 100% of the process. Depending on the complexity and volume of the process, automation of between 80 and 95% of cases would be deemed acceptable. The remaining cases are the ones that are flagged for a human operator to deal with.

BUILDING A CoE

The Center of Excellence (CoE) is discussed in conjunction with automation projects. The requirement for a CoE is very simple:

- To assist in the identification of processes to be automated,
- To help 'code' the automation - build the bots,
- To make changes to the bots when business changes occur,
- To manage the 'health' of the Bots.

The CoE considers all aspects of the RPA development: the system by which RPA happens (which software is the best fit for the organization—there are choices and the CoE would evaluate the pros and cons of the choices), identification of needs and processes through process mapping, the key employees and who will be responsible for the different aspects of the Digital Workers, their upkeep, etc. The CoE ties it all together. The CoE plans for the proper infrastructure and identifies the people with the knowledge needed to achieve the plan.

Success of any endeavor has to have a way to be evaluated. The CoE will identify the reports and expectations to measure success. It will also spell out who is responsible for coding or making additions or changes to the RPA. The CoE is the marriage of the business who know the job requirements to the people mapping it all for coding purposes (which can easily be outsourced). The CoE will conceptually make a determination to hire someone to manage the project, use someone internally, or follow a hybrid model.

As complicated as the explanation may sound, the planning is leading to the autonomic function that the Digital Worker will become. The human brain is an incredible thing. The part of the brain responsible for the autonomic processes, like breathing, swallowing, the heart beating doesn't have to be told to work. You don't have to sit and think about every breath you take or will every heartbeat or prompt every swallow. These things just happen, and when you think to control them it seems weird. It's a great thing the brain controls these functions, and the Digital Worker can fill this role in an organization with the proper planning.

Chapter 12

Why Lanshore?

Lanshore is a forward-thinking digital process consultancy, managed service provider and outsourcer, with deep knowledge and experience in robotic process automation across a range of industries. Our people and skills are the powerhouse behind the scenes of many Fortune 500 organizations. A global company, we have staff in EMEA and the Americas and a unique Robotic Operations Center of Excellence where we continually innovate, train, test, and optimize skills and technology.

Lanshore didn't start with RPA. We were a total pay commissions management company working with the mathematics of checks, helping companies go further than just how and when to pay by teaching them how to utilize, with monetary and non-monetary, reward systems. Twenty years ago, we had a vision for maximizing our clients' commissions systems so they could make more money and accomplish their goals for growth.

Working with larger partners, developing software, and utilizing commission software, it became obvious that artificial intelligence was going to impact credit card processing and pay management. AI wasn't going to affect our core offering, but to stay abreast of new trends, Lanshore started investigating how to integrate AI and machine learning into the commission's world. It became clear people weren't ready for specific AI, but RPA and attended bots were a great base for transitioning the role of advancing technology in business.

The biggest selling point for entering the world of RPA was the ability to leverage the technology for better performance and the experience RPA would create for our clientele and their organizations. Lanshore's approach centers on building companies on the forefront of digital transformation. Immersing ourselves into the world of RPA, AI, and machine learning (ML) was a natural progression for advancing our clients and ourselves. No one wants to be behind the trends, so we work hard to make sure our clients are always progressing forward, preferably ahead of their competitors.

Understanding RPA is the starting point for the journey into AI, large and small organizations can start adopting RPA in bite-size portions while expanding the Digital Worker's reach into their repertoire for success. Competitors will get there, and leaders are always looking for the leg up on their competition. Lanshore made it a company wide mission to ensure our clients are automating algorithmic tasks to free up their human capital for more objective tasks than copy pasting and comparing spreadsheets all day.

We believe digital transformation is a wholistic approach to efficiency and expanding business goals. The optimized Digital Worker will manage data interactions while human interactions and relationship building within organizations is now a focus for the humans with the data managed. It cyclically works out that the important functions are all covered and growing with a smaller margin of error and more attention to detail. Digital Workers create win-win situations for the organizations, their employees, and their clientele/constituents.

We have worked to make RPA affordable for small to mid-sized business with botsbythehour.com, which allows organizations to build, pick, or manage bots. Lanshore has worked with leading global organizations, delivering complex and large-scale robotic automation projects for years. Our Bots by the Hour products and services bring the same sophisticated and agile capabilities to individuals and smaller, leaner organizations who want to achieve competitive advantages through efficiency and fast delivery, but don't want to support and operate their own complex systems and IT infrastructure.

Our "pay for what you use" model gives you structured set-up, build and monitoring of your automated processes, delivered by our Robotic Operations Center experts. We take care of the process operation so you can focus on thought leadership and truly value-added work, while saving money through more efficient processing. This removes barriers to entry for organizations that don't have tech departments to manage larger RPA systems within the organization. The choice of bots and processes allows organizations to experience the benefits of RPA comfortably while staying within a budget. The return on investment using this route is a good way to gain proficiency and familiarity with how RPA works.

Our Robotic Operations Center (ROC) is a blueprint for successful process automation testing. We've pioneered and nurtured leading technology skills and knowledge in Robotic Process Automation (RPA), Machine Learning (ML) and human behavior emulation. Because we specialize in automation using these gateway technologies, we have our own lab environment where we test out automation instances for our clients before deploying them live. This removes risk by optimizing the processes and bots before deployment.

As a global company, we have over 130 staff in EMEA and the Americas and a unique Robotic Operations Center of Excellence where we continually innovate, train, test and optimize skills and technology.

PRACTICING WHAT WE PREACH

Automation is always growing rapidly, Lanshore has a unique perspective since we build Digital Workers, and as we leverage internally and continue to scale. Our testing of different RPA as its built teaches us which systems are incredible at different operations. Our goal is always to implement the best features, so our Digital Workers do multiple things successfully. The great thing about Lanshore taking the onus of responsibility for the performance of our creations is we put a lot of time in with the software being built.

Our human resource department utilizes a Digital Worker in the onboarding and offboarding process. We also have a skimmer that goes through the resumes that are emailed in from different recruitment websites. This Digital Worker knows the criteria we look for initially to hire and will flag the resumes that meet certain expectations. While our HR hiring leaders will still look through the resumes submitted. There are more steps the Digital Worker can take to help the process, but we won't give away all the trade secrets. Digital Workers are amazing clerically and can send immediate responses or requests for more information. RPA responses can be applied to all email and online submission-based functions. Follow-up is always important and can be set up several ways, it is no different in the hiring process and scheduling for interviews.

Lanshore uses RPA in our financial department having automated invoice creation and cross-checking different financial data. We use our own payroll and CRM software.

The best way to learn is through experience. Lanshore has the experience. As we continue to innovate and create in the technology space, we adapt and adopt. Then, we bring the most cutting-edge possibilities to our clients so they can reap the benefits of our team's dedication to success and advancement in the tech world. Our commitment to excellence is proven every time we meet with a client and begin the journey to their organization's digital future.

If you would like to see how Lanshore can advance your organizational goals, you can reach us through the 'Contact Us' option on lanshore.com or email us directly at info@lanshore.com.

Lanshore History

Lanshore started as a company that focused on monetary and non-monetary rewards for employee performance. Specifically, installing systems to help calculate, report, and generate workflow for large scale sales organizations. Over the years Lanshore began to morph into what it is now, by investigating how to institute artificial intelligence into the sales and human behavior programs. We have been working with organizations from Fortune 500 to government to institute systems and processes that help them do everything from calculate commissions to determine the time to release a prisoner.

Lanshore started as a company in 2012 that was focused on developing software applications in oil and gas, call center and commissions. The initial group worked heavily in energy trade and risk management, commission and call center management. Lanshore originally started out with offices in both Houston and San Jose, Costa Rica. In 2014 Lanshore expanded to the UK and now has offices in Glasgow along with Houston and Costa Rica.

Lanshore has software partnerships with several vendors, namely, Microsoft, Blue Prism, SAP and UiPath. Furthermore, Lanshore has partnerships with other established organizations. Over the years, Lanshore has been asked to provide first and second level support for several software companies along with developing software and architectures for their key platforms.

Lanshore's government group and clientele lists are confidential, but we can consult upon request.

The original premise of Lanshore was to create a value-based organization for our customers that incorporated aspects of both Nearshoring and Onshoring. Expert services provide out of the USA and support services from Costa Rica. As we have grown, our team has a more inclusive structure by which we function as teams and not GEO's.

Lanshore is owned by 3 partners: Douglas Erb, Mark Warne, and Elizabeth Dennett.

LANSHORE METHODOLOGY:

We're very conscious of minimizing cost to our customers: often you have already invested substantial amounts to put these systems in place and educate your people on how to use them. We don't come in with the intention to replace everything – our approach is pragmatic and economical.

Next, we draw up pictures of your current state and your future state vision. This means we can identify gaps and pain points that exist between the two. With this clear shared view, we can move forward together to correct or implement new processes and technology as needed.

Methodology steps:

- Empathize and understand
- Catalog
- Draw and agree

- New product or technology introduction (NPI/NTI)
- Acquire and implement
- Test, train and transition (unit, system, user)
- Change management
- Run and govern

Process Definition Document

This documenting process is created with inspiration from UiPath's information in mind, so there may be some crossover with their documents.

Client-Process Name

Table of Contents

I. Introduction

I.1 Purpose of the document

The Process Definition Document outlines the business process chosen for automation using Robotic Process Automation (RPA) technology. This document is to describe the manual process that is to be automated, as well as the conditions and requirements prior to its automation. This document serves as a base documentation for developers to collect the details required for robotic automation of the same process.

The document describes the sequence of steps performed as part of the business process, the conditions, and rules of the process prior to automation and how they are envisioned to work after automating it, partly or entirely. This specifications document serves as a base for developers, providing them with the details required for applying robotic process automation to the selected business process.

I.2 RPA Delivery Proces

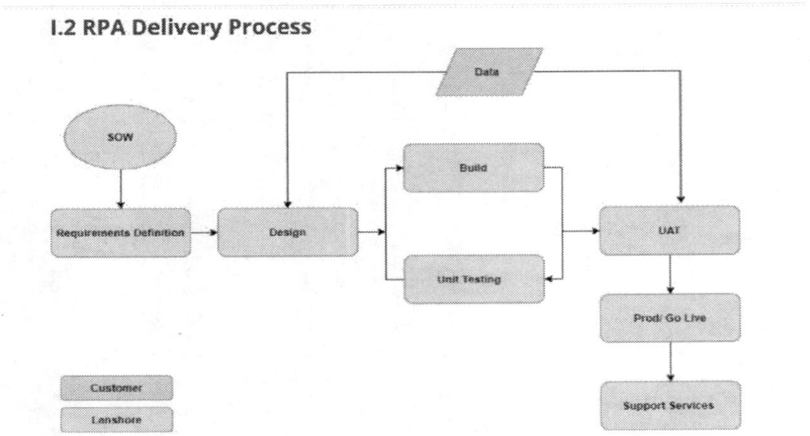

I.3 Objectives

The business objectives and benefits expected by the Business Process Owner after automation of the selected business process area:

- *{Objective 1}*
- *{Objective 2}*

I.4 Process key contact

The specifications document includes concise and complete requirements of the business process, and it is built based on the inputs provided by the **process Subject Matter Expert (SME)/ Process Owner.**

The **Process Owner** is expected **to review it and provide signoff for accuracy** and completion of the steps, context, impact, and a set of process exceptions. The details of the **Process Owner** are to be included in the table below.

Role	Name	Contact details (email, phone number)	Notes
Role	Name Last Name	Email Phone number	Time zone
Role	Name Last Name	Email Phone number	Time zone

I.5 Minimum Pre-requisites for automation

1. *A filled in Process Definition Document*
2. *User access and creation of user accounts (licenses, permissions, restrictions to create accounts for robots)*
3. *Test Data to support development*

II. As-Is process description

II.1 Process Overview

General information about the process selected for RPA prior to automation.

#	Item	Description
1	**Process full name**	TBD
2	**Process Area**	TBD
3	**Department**	TBD
4	**Process short description (operation, activity, outcome)**	TBD
5	**Role(s) required for performing the process**	TBD
6	**Process schedule and frequency**	TBD
7	**# of items processed /reference period**	TBD
8	**Process execution time**	--Average time spend per case
9	**Peak period (s)**	TBD
10	**Transaction Volume During Peak period**	TBD
11	**Total # of FTEs supporting this activity**	TBD
12	**Expected increase of volume in the next reference period**	TBD
13	**Level of exception rate**	Based on cases processed, which is the error percentage by period
14	**Input data**	TBD
15	**Output data**	TBD

*Add more rows to the table to include relevant data for the automation process. No fields should be left empty. Use "n/a" for the items that don`t apply to the selected business process.

II.2. Applications used in the process

The table includes a comprehensive list of all the applications that are used as part of the process to be automated to perform the given steps in the flow.

#	Application name & version	System Language	Thin/Thick Client	Environment/ Access method	Comments
1	Application1				
2	Application2				

*Add more rows to the table to include the complete list of applications.
Thin client - Automation of an application (windows, web, etc.) on server or remote desktop is thin client automation.
Thick client - Automation of any application, if the application is on local system, is thick client automation.

Thin client - Automation of an application (windows, web, etc.) on server or remote desktop is thin client automation. Thick client - Automation of any application, if the application is on local system, is thick client automation.

II.3 As-Is Process map

High Level As-Is Process Map:

This depicts the As-Is business process at a High Level to enable developers to have a high-level understanding of the current process.

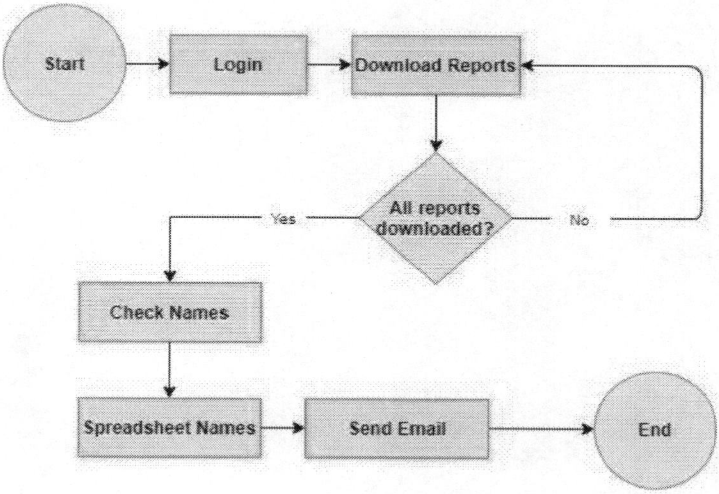

II.4 Process statistics

II. 4.1 High level statistics

II. 4.1 High level statistics

Processes	Windows	Steps	Mouse clicks	Keys pressed	Text entries	Hotkeys used	Time

*Add more rows to the table to include the complete list of applications.

II. 4.2 Detailed statistics

Window name	Mouse Clicks	Text entries	Keys pressed

*Add more rows to the table to include the complete list of applications.

II.5 Detailed Automation Process Steps

Process Initiation:

1. Step 1
2. Step 2
3. Step 3

1. Step 1

1.1 Description

Insert picture 1	Action: Details

1.2 Description

Insert picture 2	Action: Details

2. Step 2

2.1 Description

Insert picture 3	Action: Details

2.2 Description

Insert picture 4	Action: Details

III.1 Business Exceptions Handling

The Business Process Owner and Business Analysts are expected to document below all the business exceptions identified for the automation process. These can be classified as:

Known	Unknown
Previously encountered. A scenario is defined with clear actions and workarounds for each case.	New situation never encountered before. It can be caused by external factors. Cannot be predicted with precision, however if it occurs, it must be communicated to an authorized person for evaluation.

*Add more rows to the table to include the complete list of applications.

III.1.1 Known Exceptions

The table below reflects all the business process exceptions encountered during the process evaluation and documentation. These are **known exceptions** that occurred before. For each of these exceptions, define a corresponding expected action that the robot should complete if it encounters the exception.

BE #	Exception name	Step	Parameters	Action to be taken

*Add more rows to the table to include the complete list of applications.

III.1.2 Unknown Exceptions

For all other unanticipated or unknown business (process) exceptions, the robot should:

III.2 Application Error and Exception Handling

A comprehensive list of all errors, warnings or notifications should be consolidated here with the description and action to be taken, for each, by the robot.
Errors identified in the automation process can be classified as:

Area	Known	Unknown
Technology/Applications	Experienced previously, an action plan or a workaround available.	Never encountered before or may happen independently of the applications used in the process.

III.2.1 Known Errors or Exceptions

The table below reflects all the errors identified in the process evaluation and documentation.
For each of these errors or exceptions, define a corresponding expected action that the robot should complete if it is encountered.

#	Error name	Step	Parameters	Action to be taken
1	Application Crash / Internal Server Error	Any step	Error message	Recover & retry for maximum 3 times. Close the applications and run the sequence again

III.2.2 Unknown Errors and Exceptions

For all the other unanticipated or unknown application exceptions/errors, the robot should:

III.3 Reporting

#	Report type	Update frequency	Details	Monitoring Tool to visualize the data
1	Process logs	Daily	How many times was this process run since the beginning of the month and what was the average run duration?	Kibana
2	Process logs	Monthly	How many robots worked on this process per each month?	Csv file posted daily on share drive
3	Transaction logs	Daily	How many transactions were run by this process since the beginning of the month and what was the average transaction duration?	Kibana
4	Error logs	Daily	Average number of errors by type per day	Kibana
5	Error logs	Daily	All errors per month grouped by type	Csv file posted daily on drive

* For complex reporting requirements, include them into a separate document and attach it to the present documentation

III. Other Observations

Include below any other relevant observations you consider needed to be documented here.

Example: Specific Business monitoring requirements (audit and reporting) etc

IV. Additional sources of process documentation

If there is additional material created to support the process automation please mention it here, along with the supported documentation provided.

Additional Process Documentation		
Video Recording of the process (Optional)		
Standard Operating Procedure (s) (Optional)		
Business Rules Library (Optional)		
Other documentation (Optional)		

*Add more rows to the table to reflect the complete documentation provided to support the RPA process.

Risk assessment	
Percentage of compliance deficiencies or errors	Based on cases processed, which is the error percentage by month
Cases per month that don't meet SLA	How many cases per month are late base on internal SLAs?
Is the company prepared to respond to extreme events?	What happens with an unexpected increment of transactions, will the company be able to meet the customers expectations?
Based on the last question, is there an extra cost for the company?	How much extra FTEs is going to take?
How many cases are completed per month?	---Average cases completed per month
How much time does a person spend on each case	---Average time spend per case

*Add more rows to the table to reflect the complete documentation provided to support the RPA process.

NOTES

Chapter 1

1. Leinhard, John H. *Inventing the Internet.* Audio episode 1059 transcript. https://www.uh.edu/engines/epi1059.htm
2. James, Geoffrey. *31 Hilariously Bad High-Tech Predictions.* December 2015. https://www.inc.com/geoffrey-james/31-hilariously-bad-high-tech-predictions.html
3. Lee, Jindou. *Paper in a digital world: Time to eliminate the inefficiency and waste.* https://www.cio.com/article/3149529/paper-in-a-digital-world-time-to-eliminate-the-inefficiency-and-waste.html

Chapter 2

1. Moore, Susan. *Gartner Says Worldwide Robotic Process Automation Software Market Grew 63% in 2018.* Press release: Egham, U.K., June 24, 2019. https://www.gartner.com/en/newsroom/press-releases/2019-06-24-gartner-says-worldwide-robotic-process-automation-sof
2. *Deloitte Global RPA Survey: Third Annual.* https://www2.deloitte.com/bg/en/pages/technology/articles/deloitte-global-rpa-survey-2018.html

3. Abbattista, Anthony, et al. *Future smart: Why robotics changes everything.* https://www2.deloitte.com/us/en/pages/finance/articles/cfo-insights-future-smart-robotics.html

Chapter 3

1. Lanshore White Paper. *Profit Today from RPA in HR Operations: Real-World Savings, Efficiencies and Advantage from Robotic Automation.* May 2019.

Chapter 4

1. *Profit today from RPA in HR Operations: Real-World Savings, Efficiencies and Advantage from Robotic Automation.* Lanshore White Paper. May 2019.
2. *Current Fraud Statistics.* Business Fraud Prevention, Inc. https://businessfraudprevention.org/fraud-statistics/
3. Perri, Frank S. and Edyta M. Mieczkowska. *'I didn't intend to deceive anyone:' Fraud rationalizations and the guilty mind.* March/April 2015, Fraud Magazine.

Chapter 5

1. "Jordan Peterson - What Kind of Job Fits Your IQ?"

YouTube, 25 May 2021, youtu.be/P2mxdrTP-os.
2. Gregory, Hamilton. McNamara's Boys. Spring 2017.
https://www.historynet.com/mcnamaras-boys.htm

Chapter 6

1. https://www.census.gov/newsroom/press-releases/2015/cb15-97.html
2. *Total Welfare Spending Equates to $168 Per Day for Every Household in Poverty.* 7 December 2012. https://www.budget.senate.gov/newsroom/budget-background/total-welfare-spending-equates-to-168-per-day-for-every-household-in-poverty
3. Marabella, Jessica. *Is Your Local Government Ready for the Silver Tsunami?* https://www.civicplus.com/blog/hr/is-your-local-government-ready-for-the-silver-tsunami
4. Corbett, Erin. *The Officers Who Killed George Floyd Have Done This Before — Many Times.* 29 May 2020. https://www.refinery29.com/en-us/2020/05/9846650/minneapolis-police-derek-chauvin-history-force

Chapter 7

1. Makary, Dr. Michael and Michael Daniel (co-author of study). *Study Suggests Medical Errors Now Third Leading Cause of Death in the U.S.* 3 May 2016. https://www.hopkinsmedicine.org/news/media/releases/study_suggests_medical_errors_now_third_leading_cause_of_death_in_the_us
2. Sipherd, Ray. *The third-leading cause of death in US most doctors don't want you to know about*. 22 May 2018. https://www.cnbc.com/2018/02/22/medical-errors-third-leading-cause-of-death-in-america.html
3. LeverageRx. *2019 Medical Malpractice Payout Report: A complete analysis of medical malpractice payouts as recorded by the National Practitioner Data Bank.* https://www.leveragerx.com/malpractice-insurance/2019-medical-malpractice-report/

Chapter 8

1. Buck, Andrew. *57 Amazon Statistics Sellers Need to Know.* 2 November 2020. https://landingcube.com/amazon-statistics/
2. Langewiesche, William. *What Really Brought Down the Boeing 737 Max?* 18 September 2019. https://www.nytimes.com/2019/09/18/magazine/boeing-737-max-crashes.html

3. Simonite, Tom. *Intel Puts the Brakes on Moore's Law*. 23 March 2016. https://www.technologyreview.com/2016/03/23/8768/intel-puts-the-brakes-on-moores-law/
4. *A Desktop Quantum Computer for Just $5,000*. 29 January 2021. https://www.discovermagazine.com/technology/a-desktop-quantum-computer-for-just-usd5-000

Chapter 9

1. Crane, Leland D., et al. *Business Exit During the COVID-19 Pandemic: Non-Traditional Measures in Historical Context.* Finance and Economics Discussion Series Divisions of Research & Statistics and Monetary Affairs: Federal Reserve Board, Washington, D.C. April 2021. https://www.federalreserve.gov/econres/feds/files/2020089r1pap.pdf
2. Brooks, Khristopher J. *9 million U.S. small businesses fear they won't survive pandemic.* 10 February 2021. https://www.cbsnews.com/news/small-business-federal-aid-pandemic/
3. Kahlon, Param. *How automation can make sustained remote work a reality.* 26 May 2021 https://www.benefitspro.com/2021/05/26/how-automation-can-make-sustained-remote-work-a-reality/?slreturn=20210716014247

4. Waters, Richard. *Businesses turn to software robots for office work.* Originally Printed in the Financial Times, 2018. Accessed from https://www.uipath.com/newsroom/financial-times-businesses-turn-to-software-robots

Chapter 10

1. Deloitte. *The Robots are Ready. Are You? Untapped Advantage in Your Digital Workforce.* https://www2.deloitte.com/bg/en/pages/technology/articles/deloitte-global-rpa-survey-2018.html
2. Deloitte. *From brawn to brains: The impact of technology on jobs in the UK.* https://www2.deloitte.com/uk/en/pages/growth/articles/from-brawn-to-brains--the-impact-of-technology-on-jobs-in-the-u.html
3. Deloitte. *The robots are ready. Are you? Untapped advantage in your digital workforce.* https://www2.deloitte.com/bg/en/pages/technology/articles/deloitte-global-rpa-survey-2018.html

Chapter 11

1. *The robots are waiting: Are you ready to reap the benefits?* https://www2.deloitte.com/content/dam/Deloitt

e/uk/Documents/consultancy/deloitte-uk-the-robots-are-waiting.pdf

2. Tornbohm, Cathy and Roy Arup. *Competitive Landscape: Consulting and System Integration Service Providers for Robotic Process Automation*. 9 August 2018. https://www.gartner.com/en/documents/3885968

Doug's Suggested Reading List

- *Undoing Project* by Michael Lewis
- *Noise: A Flaw in Human Judgment* by Daniel Kahneman
- *Better: A Surgeon's Notes on Performance* by Atul Gawande
- *Thinkertoys: A Handbook of Creative-Thinking Techniques* (2nd Edition) by Michael Michalko
- *Freakonomics: A Rogue Economist Explores the Hidden Side of Everything* by Steven D. Levitt and Stephen J. Dubner
- *Thinkins, Fast and Slow* by Daniel Kahneman
- *Deep Reinforcement Learning Hands-On: Apply modern RL methods to practical problems of chatbots, robotics, discrete optimization, web automation, and more (*2nd Edition) by Maxim Lapan
- *Blink: The Power of Thinking Without Thinking* by Malcolm Gladwell
- *The Hitchhiker's Guide to the Galaxy* by Douglas Adams
- Anything Hemingway
- Anything Michael Lewis

Mark's Suggested Reading List

- *Machine Learning in Business: An introduction to the world of data science* by John C. Hull.
- *Robotic Process Automation using UiPath Studio X: A Citizen Developer's Guide to Hyperautomation* by Adeel Javed, Anum Sundrani, Nadia Malik and Sidney Madison Prescott.
- *The Future is Faster than You Think: How Converging Technologies are Transforming Business, Industry and Our Lives* (Exponential Technology Series) by Peter H. Diamandis and Steven Kotler.

Elizabeth's Suggested Reading List

- *Crossing The Chasm*, by Geoffrey Moore
- *Algorithms to Live By: The Computer Science of Human Decisions*, by Brian Christian
- *Zero to One,* by Peter Thiel and Blake Masters
- *How To Win Friends and Influence People,* by Dale Carnegie
- *Why Digital Transformations Fail - The Surprising Disciplines of How to Take Off and Stay Ahead,* by Tony Saldanha
- *Hello World: How to Be Human in the Age of the Machine*, by Hannah Fry

Author and Co-Contributor Bios

Douglas Erb

Doug Erb was born in the steel mill town of Highland Indiana. He led a fairly normal life as a child, doing traditional things like playing baseball, football, and eating at Subway. During his formative years, he decided to take a machine shop class. It was in this class that his life path would be set. In woodshop class, Mr. Erb got into a fight with another student. The shop teacher promptly picked Mr. Erb and the other student up by the arm and threw him against the wall. At this point, Mr. Erb decided he would switch from shop classes to Home Economics. In doing this, one of his first classes was typing. While his grades were terrible as a typist, it was this foundation that allowed him to become more proficient in college than most students, and hence faster when writing and developing. He also had a thirst for math, which in general came easy.

When Doug went to University, he graduated with a Bachelor's degree at Indiana State University. Upon graduating from ISU, Doug began his career teaching others how to use technology then graduated to working with organizations that were utilizing technology in the pay and time tracking fields. He decided to get a master's degree in MIS at University of Houston Clear Lake, and it was there he met his first mentor, Professor Van Tran. It was Dr. Tran who convinced Doug to get into programming SAP, which led to Mr. Erb's first consulting opportunity at Andersen Consulting (now Accenture).

Over the years, he has had the opportunity to work with many different companies solving issues that were largely focused on sales and human behavior as it applies to monetary and non-monetary rewards. Having worked solving issues that apply to data cleansing, business intelligence, and general guidance for organizations, Mr. Erb has had his hands in architecting sophisticated systems for companies from SMB to Fortune 500. His handy work can still be observed today at companies such as T-Mobile, MicroFocus, and others.

Many years ago, while attending an IBM conference on AI, he got a thirst for how decisions and the data that impact them could be cleaner and used to answer more sophisticated questions with a higher degree of certainty in the results in the field of human behavior. It was here he started to learn more about AI, and how to take customers from low education on AI to full adoption. This is where his model for process automation to decision automation came to fruition.

Mark Warne

Mark Warne is a Partner at Lanshore LLC and has worked extensively in the fields of Energy, Sales Performance Management, and Disruptive Technologies, such as Artificial Intelligence, Machine Learning, and Robotic Process Automation. Mark spent many years working at an Exploration and Production company as well as an Energy Transportation Company before moving to Altra Energy Technologies LLC in the middle of the dotcom boom. Mark has continued to work and consultant in the area of information technology since that time.

Mark has a Bachelor of Commerce from the University of Calgary and a Master of Business Administration from Athabasca University. At the time of publishing this book, Mark held a Chartered Professional Accountant (CPA CMA) designation in the province of Alberta Canada.

Although he grew up in Canada, Mark lives in Houston Texas with his wife, Claudia, and their two Texas born ice hockey playing children.

Ben Cordner

Ben is Lanshore's Solutions Architect with a solid understanding of RPA and expertise in delivering complex projects on platforms from numerous vendors. He has a background in integration engineering and research science making him a trained problem solver with an analytical mind and an organized, methodical approach to professional challenges. Ben is a known self-starter accustomed to taking initiative, managing large workloads, and meeting deadlines. His confident and dynamic character forges strong working relationships while still operating effectively as part of teams.

Ben's notable work includes Her Majesty's Revenue and Customs (HMRC) was one of the first UK government departments to realize the potential of RPA. The finances released in order to automate the processing of all manner of online tax forms and inquires was approximately £20m. This effort was split between numerous RPA vendors and third-party solution providers. Ben provided expert guidance as a representative of one of the RPA vendors to those third parties including best practices and performance optimization.

Unity Media, a German telco now merged with Vodafone, was undergoing a customer interaction transformation project with RPA. Ben developed the principal automations for subscription cancellations and the changing of bank account details which included automated communication with Unity Media's customers. He successfully assisted Unity Media in establishing their own in-house RPA center of excellence which, with guidance, subsequently rolled out numerous additional process automations.

Bouygues Telecom, a major French telco invited numerous RPA vendors to perform PoCs so they could select a vendor to deliver their back-office automation transformation. Ben was selected as the individual to represent the vendor and build the PoC which entailed working onsite for 3 months, performing business analysis, process selection, and automation development.

With his physics, mathematics, and biology background and various capabilities with all thing's tech, Ben is able to adapt to many companies and see what can be most effective for them with ease.

Elizabeth Dennett

Elizabeth graduated from the University of Leeds with a Material Science and Engineering Degree. Whilst at University, she gained a place on the BOC Group Graduate Management training scheme where she spent the next 3 years. Moving into IT, Elizabeth joined the US based software company, Computer Associates, working in sales and technical roles, in infrastructure management, and security. During this time, Elizabeth was accepted to study for an MBA at the University of Warwick. Elizabeth became Vice President at CA before leaving to join IBM, initially working as a sales leader in the IT security space. Whilst at IBM, Elizabeth had both of her children, and enjoyed maternity leave and flexible working. Returning from the birth of her second daughter, she moved from a strategy role into Business Analytics and Sales Performance management.

After nearly 20 years in large IT companies, Elizabeth wanted a new challenge and left IBM. Within less than a month, she was introduced to Doug Erb by an ex-IBM colleague. She joined Canidium then came with Doug to Lanshore. Elizabeth has run the European operation from the beginning and worked as part of the global leadership team, 2 years ago picking up the global responsibility for marketing and business development. Whilst at Lanshore, Elizabeth continued the focus in SPM but has enjoyed the move into RPA, which is underpinned by her diverse IT and business background and experience.

Elizabeth is passionate about creating a blended working environment which allows everybody to maintain a healthy work life balance.

Made in the USA
Monee, IL
04 November 2026

67386077R10114